THE COMPLETE

WIN AT SPADES

Joseph D. Andrews

BONUS BOOKS, INC.
Chicago, Illinois

THE UNITED STATES PLAYING CARD COMPANY
Cincinnati, Ohio
www.usplayingcard.com

04   03   02   01   00   5   4   3   2   1

Library of Congress Control Number: 00-106139

ISBN: 1-56625-145-1 (Bonus Books edition)
ISBN: 1-889752-09-6 (USPC edition)

Bonus Books, Inc.
160 East Illinois Street
Chicago, Illinois 60611

The United States Playing Card Company
4590 Beech Street
Cincinnati, Ohio 45212

Printed in the United States of America

This book is dedicated to my five dear sisters —
Patti Ann, Maureen, Pauline, Susan and Heidi

Table of Contents

Table of Contents

Listing of Illustrative Hands

PREFACE

SPADES IS A WONDERFUL (AND NOW CLASSIC) GAME, HAVING DESCENDED
from Whist and Bridge. It first appeared in the late 1930s, was popu-
larized during the Second World War, and eventually found its way to
college campuses. It is now the most popular four-handed card game on
the Internet — outdistancing Bridge and Hearts combined! Spades is
usually played as a partnership game; however, there is an individual's
variation for three and four persons! It is a deceptively easy game to
learn — but don't let the simplicity of the rules fool you! Like Chess
or Bridge, you can be playing in an hour — but it requires many
months of practice and improvement to become an accomplished
player.

Partnership Spades is the ideal team competition. The application of
skill in interpreting the meaning of your opponents' bids and plays is the
key to success. You and your partner work together — bidding the optimum contracts, playing hands cooperatively, and utilizing sound
defensive technique. Part of the fascination of the game of Spades is the
Nil bid — in which the emphasis is on making *zero* tricks in a given
hand. Another interesting feature is the "bag" rule in which the unfortunate player who makes overtricks is penalized. Finally the "set" or defeat
of any contract results in the reduction of points!

This book will teach you the basics of the game if you are a novice
player. For those with more experience, *Win At Spades* is a valuable tool
for improving bidding, play of the hand, and defensive skills. Your game
will move to a higher level! Several illustrative hands feature instructive

themes or truly unusual plays. A number of experts have contributed useful and interesting material — including material referencing the many variations of the game. A chapter listing popular Internet Sites and related information has been included. Perhaps someday you will compete for a National Championship at a "live" event — or "swim" with the biggest sharks on the Internet! And the best part is that you will have your own teeth to bite back!

— *Joe Andrews, Summer 1999*

PROLOGUE

THE MODERN GAME OF SPADES BECAME POPULAR IN THE LATE 1940S, especially on college campuses. It is difficult to ascertain the true origin of this game. A review of several card game reference sources revealed that Spades descended directly from Whist. Spades also has a kindred spirit with Bridge, Pinochle, Euchre, and other similar games featuring partnership play, bidding, and a trump suit. George Coffin, the great Bridge author, traced the roots of Spades to the midwest. He determined that this game was introduced in Cincinnati sometime between 1937 and 1939. From there, it spread to other cities in the general region, and eventually into the military. Spades was played extensively during World War II, as it was a fast-paced game which could be interrupted at any time — especially during battle conditions! Please note that (the late) Mr. Coffin completed extensive research relative to the history of many card games. At one time, he was the most prolific Bridge writer in the country and competed against some of the greatest players of his era. (1930-70).

In the olden days of Whist, some chap disliked having to turn his last card as dealer to determine trump. He would find it to be a singleton, while holding seven cards of another suit, perhaps, A K Q J XXX. To avoid such quirks of chance, this bright chap introduced the dealer's right to declare his best suit for trump. Later, another player conceived the idea of *bridging* to his partner the privilege to name trump. Next came Bid Whist, a competitive auction, and the option for a "declarer" to play the hand. However, Whist had been in a steady decline for several years. In 1925, the late Harold S. Vanderbilt created the game of Contract Bridge.

The key feature of his innovation was the fact that you could not score game unless you had bid it. In addition, Vanderbilt added special bonuses for successfully bid and made slams (12 or 13 tricks). Soon, Ely Culbertson created additional features that helped to make Bridge the outstanding game it is. Charles Goren, a Philadelphia lawyer really moved the game to the echelons of popularity with his Sports Illustrated columns, TV shows, and "Standard American Point Count Bidding System". Later the innovation of the Duplicate formate elevated Bridge to its highest level.

Another trail blazer, Alfred Sheinwold, wrote a daily syndicated newspaper column and a classic Bridge book entitled FIVE WEEKS TO WINNING BRIDGE (1957). The ACBL* enjoyed phenomenal growth into the 1970s. Today, Bridge still has a huge following of devotees and a wonderful network of dedicated directors.

Meanwhile, Spades continued its steady growth. After the Second World War, it became established nationally. It is now the number one card game in colleges as well as in the military services. The appeal of Spades is the relatively basic bidding system, opportunity for partnership play, and the fast paced action. It is an easy game to learn, but it requires several months or years of practice and experience to become an accomplished player.

There is also a fertile ground for advanced techniques. Many Bridge players have "cut their eye teeth" on Spades — which is now the most popular four-handed card game on the Internet. More than twenty-five thousand players enjoy Spades every day at several Sites, and it exceeds the volume of Bridge and Hearts combined! (A review of some of the more popular Internet "hangouts"is featured later in this article.) The popularity of Spades is ensured as the Internet becomes more and more accessible. Eventually, a series of "live" tournaments and a national rating system will allow anyone to seek a competitive game — locally and regionally.

For more information, refer to the Internet Chapter of this book.

---

* American Contract Bridge League (Memphis, TN)

A GLOSSARY OF TERMS

AUCTION — The interval in which the bidding occurs.

BAG(S) — Additional trick(s) over and above a specific bid (e.g., a bid of five making seven would yield two bags). Note — Each bag, per se, has no penalty value; however, an accumulation of ten bags is assessed a 100 point penalty.

"BAG-EM" — A bidding system requiring each player to bid one. (Reverse Spades).

BEMO — *A bidding system which rewards a partnership for winning the first six tricks of a hand (plus 100 points).*

BID — a number from 1–13 specifying a QUANTITY of tricks a player hopes to win in a given hand. Note — a bid of nil or blind nil is a declaration to take zero tricks. The opening bid is declared by the player to the dealer's immediate left.

BLIND NIL — A bid of zero which is made before a player sees his cards. Note — a successful blind nil bid scores plus 200 points. An unsuccessful blind nil bid scores minus 200 points. In some circles a "pass" of one or two cards is exchanged after a blind nil bid. This is optional, and not recommended for competitive games.

"BRIMER'S RULE" — When the contract consists of 12 or 13 tricks, always try to "set" the opponents' bid.

BROKEN — Jargon for the playing of a spade (trump) which allows for subsequent leads of spades. Note — trumps cannot be led until a spade has been played or the player on lead has nothing but spades in his hand.

CASH — To play an established winning card (e.g., Ace of trump, or a winning card of another suit).

CLUB LEAD — The person holding the deuce of clubs (after the round of bidding is completed) must lead this card. The winner of this (first) trick, then has the first lead of the next (second) trick. (Note — This is an optional rule.)

CONTRACT — The final combined partnership bid (e.g., North bids three, South bids five, yielding a contract of eight tricks for that partnership).

CONTROL — A key high card — usually the established Ace or King of a suit.

CONVENTION — A partnership agreement denoting a specific meaning to a bid or discard.

COVER(a) — A general term describing support of your partner's nil bid by playing key high cards or trumping strategically.

COVER(b) — The play of the next immediate high card of the suit led (e.g., your right hand opponent leads the QUEEN of diamonds — if you hold the KING of diamonds, your play of this card is a "cover."

CUTTHROAT — Another term for an individual's variation of the game where each person plays "solo" instead of partnership.

DEFENDER-(DEFENSE) — The term for the partnership which attempts to defeat or set their opponents' bid. Note — each partnership has a dual function to make their own bid, and if possible, to defeat their opponents' bid.

DISCARD — The play of another suit, when void of the suit led (instead of trumping).

DOUBLETON — A term for holding exactly two cards in any suit.

DRAW — Another word referring to the cashing of winners in the trump suit (spades).

DUCK — A strategic play of a low card usually intended to avoid bags.

DUPLICATION — Equal values in the same suit distributed between a partnership (e.g., you hold in diamonds — Ace, Queen, 10, 7, 4; your partner holds in the same suite — King, Jack, 9, 6. The trick taking value here is significantly reduced as the opponents will probably trump on the second or third round).

ECHO — A suit count signal which gives a partner a reading on the length of a specific suit which you hold (e.g., you hold the 8 and 4 of clubs. On the first round, you play the 8; on the second round, you play the 4 — this indicates to your partner that you hold a doubleton in clubs and can trump on the next lead). This is sometimes called (a high-low signal).

ENCOURAGE — The play of a high card under partners high card lead of the same suit which requests partner to continue that suit.

ENDPLAY — A strategic maneuver in which an opponent is thrown into the lead at the end of a hand and is forced to make a favorable return (to your hand).

FOURS — A bidding system requiring each player to bid four tricks. The total of 16 tricks bid results in a guaranteed set for at least one of the partnerships.

ENTRY — Any card which allows access to partners hand.

"ERIN'S RULE" — Nil Bids with four small trump are best made with distributional hands (e.g. a void or singleton in a side suit.)

FINESSE — An effort to win a trick with a card which is not the highest card in a given suit (e.g., you hold the Ace and Queen of a suit while not on lead. That suit is led and you play the **Queen** hoping to win two tricks.

HOMICIDE — A bidding system in which the combined number of tricks must equal 14. This forces someone to be set or defeated.

HONOR — The Ace, King, Queen, Jack or 10 of any suit, often called honor cards.

HESITATION — An unethical or deceptive practice of intentionally delaying the play of a card in order to convey information to partner. Note — another term for this is **lagging** and usually refers to the delay of playing a card in a computer or Internet game.

HOLDUP — The intentional choice of ducking a trick which you could have won.

JOKER — A card or cards added to the deck in order to create a new variation. Jokers are ranked above the Ace of spades. (There are usually two Jokers — "big" and "small".)

LEAD — The first card played to any trick or the first play of a hand. Note — in this book, the opening leader is the player to the right of the dealer. Another variation is the lead from the left of the dealer.

LHO/RHO/OAT — Abbreviations for Left Hand Opponent; Right Hand Opponent; and Opponent Across Table. Note — "OAT" is not applicable in this edition, as the player across from you is your Partner.

LITTLE — Non-honor cards (9, and below) often called "spot cards."

LIMIT-(GAME) — Usually 500 point for partnership or 300 points for individuals. Note — some rule books have a negative limit of minus 300 points. Another variation is a specified number of hands — usually 10 per round.

LONG — Holding great length in any suit (e.g., ACE, KING, XXXX is referred to as "ACE, KING, sixth"; "ACE, QUEEN, xx" is referred to as "ACE, QUEEN, fourth".) Note — most of the combinations indicate the number of cards held in each suit.

MAJOR SUIT — Spades and hearts.

MINOR SUIT — Clubs and diamonds.

MIRROR — A bidding system in which the actual number of spades in your hand denotes your bid.

MOON — (Grand Slam — a bid to take all 13 tricks. Successful moon bids score a premium of 200 points.)

NIL — A bid of zero in which a player expects to take no tricks. A successful nil bid scores a premium of 100 points. Blind nil is also a zero bid; however, the player cannot look at his/her cards prior to making this call.

"ORPHAN" — Any spot spade (trump 2–9) which becomes established for a key trick at the end of a hand.

PENALTY — Points lost for failure to make any bid or contract; also, points deducted for the accumulation of bags in increments of ten.

PASS — In some circles, as pass of one or two cards is made between the partners after a **Blind Nil** bid. This is strictly for a fun game only.

REVOKE — Failure to follow suit whenever possible. In live games, the penalty for revoke is two tricks. Internet or computer games do not allow revoking. Note — another term for revoke is renege.

RUFF — Another word for trumping. Note — "**Overruff**" refers to playing a higher trump after a ruff. "**Underruff**" is a discard of a lower trump after a ruff on the same trick.

RUFF/SLUFF — The lead of a suit in which both opponents are void. The result is usually a discard by one opponent as the other trumps. This is considered a very poor play.

RULE OF ELEVEN — If the number of bid tricks is less than eleven, it is usually correct to "Bag" the opponents after making your bid.

SECOND HAND LOW — The practice of playing a low card in the second position after the lead. This allows partner a chance to win the trick in fourth position.

SET — The taking of less tricks than the number specified or the defeating of the opponents contract. (Synonymous with "defeat.")

SMALL SLAM — A bid of 12 tricks. If successful, the premium is 100 points.

SEQUENCE — Connected honor cards of the same suit in the same hand (e.g., King, Queen, Jack; or Ace, King, Queen; or, Queen, Jack, ten, etc.).

SINGLETON — The holding of only one card in a suit.

SQUEEZE — A forced play against an opponent who must guard two or more suits simultaneously, and thus is forced to discard a key card.

SUICIDE — A bidding system in which one member of a partnership is required to bid nil in every hand.

TABLE TALK — Jargon for any conversation about specific cards in one's hand or the meaning of a bid. This practice is both unethical and illegal.

THIRD HAND HIGH — The standard play of your highest card in the third position in order to prevent the fourth player from winning a trick with a low card.

TRUMP — The highest ranking suit which is always spades. This term is also applied to the play of a spade.

TRUMP PROMOTION — The natural progressive development of a lower ranking trump to a higher position in the same hand. This is accomplished by a series of overruffs.

UPPERCUT — The playing of a higher trump after an opponent's ruff.

VOID — Holding no cards in a given suit.

WALTER'S CONVENTION (Suit Preference lead) — The rank of the card returned for a Ruff (by partner) indicates the suit which is the entry back to your hand.

REVIEW OF BASICS

THE BASIC RULES AND PRINCIPLES OF SPADES ARE RELATIVELY SIMPLE. Please refer to the next section if you are familiar with these bare essentials.

THE PLAYERS

The standard game is four handed with two sets of partnerships playing opposite each other. There is also a three handed variation in which each person plays individually. Finally, a four handed option exists with each person playing individually although this form of the game is relatively obsolete. Although each person in the individual games plays for himself, two or more players may team up as a temporary partnership if this is advantageous for them.

THE PACK

A standard 52 card deck is used. There are four suits and the cards of each suit rank as follows:

Ace (high), King, Queen, Jack, 10, 9, and so forth down to the deuce.

Spades are always trump and outrank the other three suits. The terms major and minor are used for quick identification only. Major suits are hearts and spades; minor suits are diamonds and clubs. The ACE, KING, QUEEN, JACK, and 10 are called "honor" cards; the deuce to the nine are called "spot cards."

THE OBJECT OF THE GAME

Each partnership strives to win the highest score which is usually 500 points. This is accomplished by capturing tricks, setting or defeating the opponent's **contracts** and avoiding the accumulation of overtricks. The **standard** game limit for partnership variation is 500 points. Individual games have a limit of 300 points. There are penalties for defeated contracts, as well as the accumulation of overtricks (bags). In tournament play, the game limit is ten hands. This is designed to control the time, as well as length of each round.

SCORING

Each successful contract scores 10 points for every trick bid and made as well as one as one point for every additional trick. For example, if you bid seven, (combined partnership) and make nine (tricks), you score 70+2 for a total of 72 points. If you are unsuccessful in making your bid (set) your team loses 10 points for every trick bid. Using the above example, if your team was defeated in the contract of seven tricks the result would be minus 70 points.

Remember, partnership bids are **combined** and the total made or set is the basis of the scoring. Successful nil bids score a premium of 100 points. Defeated nil bids have a penalty of minus 100 points. Please note that a nil is an individual **contract** and the partner of the nil bidder has his or her score calculated **separately**. For example, if I bid nil and my partner bids three and we are both successful, we score plus 130 points. If my partner is set and I still make my nil bid, we score plus 70 (100 minus 30).

Any tricks taken by a nil bidder do **not** count toward the total of the other partner's bid. Successful **blind nils** have a premium of 200 points, and a defeated blind nil is penalized 200 points.

Bags are a penalty for over-conservative bidding. Every additional trick (over trick) in a successful contract counts as one bag.* An accumulation of 10 bags results in a penalty of 100 points. It is quite possible to "sit" on a total of nine bags, and not incur a penalty. Bags are sometimes called sandbags.

*(add one point).

GETTING STARTED

As stated previously the most frequently played variety of Spades is **partnership.** The first step is to draw cards for partners unless you already have a partner. The two players who have drawn the two highest cards are partners against the other two. In the event of a tie, the suits are ranked spades, hearts, diamonds and then clubs, as in the game of Bridge. The King of hearts is higher than the King of clubs, etc. Note that the ranking of suits has relevance only in this instance. Each player sits at a specific direction opposite his or her partner. This book will always use the layout shown here.

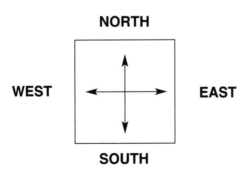

Both pairs are "teams" and compete as partnerships (North/South vs. East/West). Two decks of cards are recommended for each table. One deck is in use and the other is prepared for the next deal. If only one deck is available, that is quite acceptable. The dealer is determined by a draw of cards or mutual agreement. The deck is thoroughly shuffled and then offered to the player on the dealer's immediate right for the "cut" — which may be declined. The cards are then dealt one at a time, in a clockwise rotation until the whole deck is depleted. Each person thus receives 13 cards. It is always a good idea to count your cards — ensuring a proper deal. Any misdeal is "thrown in," and the hand is re-dealt after a new shuffle and cut.

SORTING YOUR HAND

At this point, each player sorts his or her cards in a logical fashion.

This is best accomplished by **alternating** the colored suits starting with diamonds, then clubs, hearts and finally spades on the right of your hand. The ranking of cards in each suit should be from highest to lowest. This will enable you to identify you suits and key cards more quickly. Nothing is more confusing than to have your hand sorted in a haphazard fashion which could result in a **renege** or incorrectly played card.

Here are some typical sorted hands from left to right:

♦ A 5 3   ♣ 10 9 7 2   ♥ K 3 2   ♠ J 9 6

Here is another example featuring a **void** suit:

♦ K Q J 5 3   ♠ A 7 6 5 2   ♥ Q 9 5

Note that the **spades** are placed on the **far right**, if possible, or in the middle with a void in clubs and two red suits. If void in a red suit, then start with clubs on the far left, the other red suit, and then spades. If you follow this basic plan, you will be able to proceed with your bid and play your hand more comfortably.

TRICKS (BOOKS)

The play of every deal consists of 13 tricks. Each trick is a packet or book containing four cards — one from each player's hand. Cards are played individually in a **clockwise** rotation and placed face up on the table. Remember, each player must follow in turn. For example, if East leads a card, South then plays next, followed by West, and finally North.

BRIEF OVERVIEW

There are three basic phases to every hand of Spades — **the bidding, the play, and the scoring.** There is a specific rotation of play in which each player follows a precise clockwise pattern. However, before we discuss bidding, it is necessary to understand the play first. After the deal and bidding sequence is completed, the opening leader (**the person seated to the immediate left of the dealer**) plays the first card of the hand. Trump may **not** be led until spades have been played ("**broken**") or that player has nothing left in his hand but spades. The examples illustrated below will establish a pattern for the way each trick is played.

OPENING LEAD / ROTATION OF PLAY

The person making the opening lead is seated to the left of the dealer. There are variations, such as the deuce of clubs Rule, or lead from another direction. For our purposes, we will follow the Contract Bridge Rule of the standard left-hand lead.

The opening leader now selects any card, other than a spade, and places it face-up on the table. This initiates the play of the hand. Then, in clockwise rotation, each player follows the suit led (if possible). If a player is void in the suit led, the choice is to trump with a spade, or discard a card in either of the other two suits. The highest card of the suit led (or highest trump, if applicable) wins that trick. Let us look at an illustrative example:

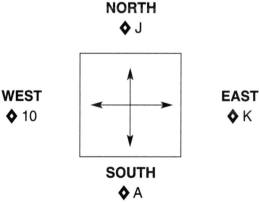

NORTH

♦ J

WEST

♦ 10

EAST

♦ K

SOUTH

♦ A

West is the dealer and the bidding has been completed. North makes the opening lead of the Jack of diamonds. East plays the King; South covers with his Ace and West plays his 10.

Note the clockwise rotation and the following play of cards in the same suit. South wins this trick, forms a book of four cards and places it face down on the table. Now South having won the last trick, makes the first lead to the next trick. Each player must follow suit if they can. If a player cannot follow the suit led, then he can either discard another suit, or trump with a spade. Here is another example:

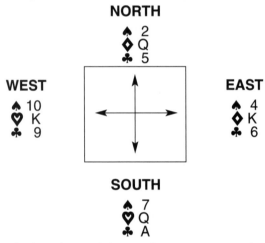

North leads the Queen of diamonds, East covers with the King, and now South has a choice. He may discard the Queen of hearts or the Ace of clubs, or may trump with his singleton spade.

Note that the Ace of clubs if discarded, does not win the trick as it is a neutral card. If South chooses not to trump, West has the option to allow his partner to win the trick with the King of diamonds. If South does choose to trump this trick, then West, who is also void of diamonds, may overruff with his spade 10. Another option for West is to make a discard of a heart or club and allow South to take the trick. Remember diamonds were played initially. This allows many options for West and South whereas East has no choice but to follow suit.

Spades (trump) is the key element of the game. Any trump, even the lowly deuce, ranks higher than any card of any other suit. If you are void of hearts and you hold the deuce of spades, you have a winner should you choose to trump (and the other two players have to follow suit). When a trick contains **two or more trump,** it is won by the person who plays the **higher or highest trump.** This applies to both the lead of trump or the use of trump to ruff a side suit.

Assume that we are at the end of the hand and these are the last two tricks. North is on lead and chooses to play the four of spades, East must play the three, South follows with the ten, and West wins with the Jack. This is straightforward and now West will win the last trick with the King of diamonds. Now let us suppose North selects the lead of the King of hearts. This changes the matrix. East may try for a spade ruff (rather than the diamond discard) and South may be tempted to overruff with the spade 10. West, also void in hearts, wins the Jack. He must then concede a trick to North's last trump. Had North chosen to lead his spade first, West would have taken two tricks. The heart lead by North allows the establishing of the spade four by having his partner force the Jack of spades with his ten. This is a theme which will be analyzed more thoroughly in the advanced Spades book. Trump promotion is a somewhat advanced technique. In Bridge books, it is called "uppercutting." Often, it will spell the difference between a successful contract or a set contract.

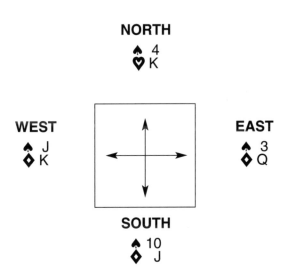

BICYCLE

4

SPADES — GENERAL
INFORMATION

THIS CHAPTER WAS CONTRIBUTED BY JOHN MCLEOD OF LONDON, England. (Reproduced with permission of the publisher.) He is one of the world's leading authorities on all card games. His site features catalogued and detailed information and a fascinating listing of card games unique to many countries. For a "fantastic card voyage" — visit the Web Page — www.pagat.com/ You will have a lot of fun!

Please note that the game of Spades is replete with many variations and Rules interpretations. Several experts have supplied information for this Section. There are plenty of references to various Spades sites. I have also opted to insert a few comments relative to the Rules — especially in reference to Tournament competition.

Spades is played quite widely in the USA, but does not seem to have spread to any other countries. It is a plain-trick game in which spades are always trumps. It is most often played as a partnership game by four players, but there are also versions for three and for two players.

The following rules rely originally on contribution from Theodore Hwa, Dennis J. Barmore — (4 player game) and Szu Kay Wong — (3 player game). Many variations have been added, contributed by John Hay, Daniel Hines, and others.

CONTENTS

Spades for Four Players
Variations of Spades for Four Players
Spades for Six Players
Spades for Three Players
Spades for Two Players
Szu Kay Wong's Advice on playing Spades, mostly for three player games.
Other Spades WWW sites

SPADES FOR FOUR PLAYERS

The four players are in fixed partnerships, with partners sitting opposite each other. Deal and play are clockwise.

RANK OF CARDS

A standard pack of 52 cards is used. The cards, in each suit, rank from the highest to lowest: A,K,Q,J,10,9,8,7,6,5,4,3,2.

THE DEAL

The first dealer is chosen at random, and the turn to deal rotates clockwise. The cards are shuffled and then dealt singly, in clockwise order beginning with the player on the dealer's left, until all 52 cards have been dealt and everyone has 13.

THE BIDDING

Each partnership must make a bid, which is the number of tricks they expect to take. It is important to realize that in Spades both sides' bids stand (it is not like other bidding games in which only the higher bid counts). First the non-dealer's side agrees on a bid. Each partner on that side communicates the amount of tricks they expect to take, based on their cards. A certain amount of unspecified bantering about "halves" and "maybes" is permitted, but not specific information about cards held. For example, you are allowed to say, "I know I can take 4 tricks, I might be able to take 6." *[In competitive events or Tournaments, this is not permissible and would be interpreted as "Table Talk".]* You are not allowed to say, "I have a couple of high hearts and a singleton in clubs." The agreed upon bid is then written down. The other side then agrees on a bid in the same manner.

Nil is a declaration that that player will not win any tricks during the play. Any single player may bid nil. The nil bidder's partner will also bid the number of tricks to be taken by the partnership.

Blind nil may be bid by a player whose side is losing by at least 100 points. It is a nil bid declared before a player looks at his cards. The bidder may exchange two cards with partner — the bidder discards two cards face down; partner picks them up and gives back two cards face-down in return.

THE PLAY OF THE HAND

On the first trick, everyone must play their lowest club. A player who has no clubs must discard a diamond or a heart. No spades may be played to the trick. On this first trick it does not matter much in what order the four players play their cards — but if you want to be fussy then the holder of the 2 of clubs should lead, and the others play in clockwise order. The trick is won by the highest club played. *[This is an alternative to having the person to the left or right of the dealer making the opening lead.]*

The player who won the first trick leads to the next. Any card except a spade may be led. Each player, in turn, clockwise, must follow suit if able; if unable to follow suit, the player may play any card. A trick containing a spade is won by the highest spade played; if no spade is played, the trick is won by the highest card of the suit led. The player who wins a trick leads to the next. Spades may not be led until:

Some player has played a spade (on the lead of another suit, of course), or the leader has nothing but spades left in hand.

Playing the first spade is known as "breaking" spades.

SCORING

A side that takes at least as many tricks as its bid calls for receives a score equal to 10 times a bid. Additional tricks (overtricks) are worth an extra one point each.

Sandbagging rule: A side which (over several deals) accumulates ten or more overtricks has 100 points deducted from its score. Any overtricks beyond ten are carried over to the next cycle of ten overtricks — that is if they reached twenty overtricks they would lose another 100 points and so on. *Note: it is not necessary to keep track of overtricks separately as the cumulative number of overtricks taken appears as the final digit of the team's score, if positive.)*

If a side does not make its bid, they lose 10 points for each trick they bid.

If a bid of **nil** is successful, the nil bidders' side receives 50 points. This is in addition to the score won (or lost) by the partner of the nil bidder for tricks made. If a bid of nil fails — that is, the bidder takes at least one trick — the bidder's side loses 50 points (but still receives any amount scored for the partner's bid, and the tricks won by the nil bidder count towards making the partner's bid).

A bid of blind nil scores twice as much as ordinary nil — it wins 100 points if successful and loses 100 points if it fails.

The side which reaches 500 points first wins the game. If both sides reach 500 points in a single deal, the side with the higher score wins.

VARIATIONS OF SPADES FOR FOUR PLAYERS

Dennis J. Barmore (sharksinc@aol.com) runs a mailing list for information about Spades, Bid Whist, and Pinochle clubs and tournaments in the United States. He has contributed the following description of a variant which is widely played by African Americans. The rules are as in basic spades (above), but with the following differences:

1. **Cards:** The game is played with a standard pack with two distinct jokers; the twos of clubs and hearts are removed from the pack leaving 52 cards. The two jokers are the highest trumps. If one is colorful and the other is plain, the colorful one is higher. If your pack has identical jokers, write "BIG" on one of them, and that one is higher.

The third highest trump is the two of spades — so the trump suit ranks: **big joker, small joker, 2,A,K,Q,J,10,9,8,7,6,5,4,3.**

2. **Leading:** After the bidding, the **dealer** leads to the first trick and may lead **any card of any suit.** Throughout the game, any card may be led to a trick. You do not have to wait for spades to be broken before leading them.

3. **Scoring:** If a team makes fewer tricks than they bid, they score minus the value of the contract — for example if you bid 8 and lose you score -80. There is no extra score for undertricks.

4. **Bidding blind:** There is no *nil* or *blind nil* bid, but a partnership may bid **blind seven,** provided neither of them has yet looked at their cards. This doubles the score to 140 if successful and -140 if not. If they make overtricks, these count one each as usual.

5. In theory it is also possible to bid higher numbers blind for double the score: **blind 8** is worth 160, **blind 9** is 180 and so on. However, such bids will not be worthwhile, except possibly when they give you just enough points to win the game if successful.

OTHER VARIATIONS

Here are some further variants, mostly contributed by Theodore Hwa. Ben Miller provided the information on No Trump and Double Nil.

VARIATIONS IN THE CARDS AND THEIR RANKING

In some versions of Spades, some or all of the four twos are elevated to the top of the spade suit, are ranked in some specified order, and are considered to be spades. The rest of the cards rank as in normal.

Spades can also be played with a 54 card pack — the standard pack of 52 plus 2 distinguishable jokers. In this case the two jokers are elevated to be the top two cards of the spade suit, with a particular order of the jokers specified. If jokers are used, then there will be two cards left over at the end of the deal, and these are given to the dealer. Having looked at all 15 cards, the dealer discards any two cards face down. Some play such that the two extra cards are given to the holder of the two of clubs rather than the dealer. Some play that the discard takes place after the bidding.

VARIATIONS IN THE BIDDING

Some play that each team must bid a minimum of 4 tricks. If a player bids nil, the player's partner must bid at least 4.

Some play such that after each partnership has agreed its initial bid, each side, beginning with the side that made the first bid, is then given the opportunity to increase its bid.

Some play that the bids of the two sides must not add up to exactly 13 tricks. This makes it impossible for both teams to win their bid exactly.

ROUND-THE-TABLE BIDDING

This is an alternative to partnership bidding. Beginning with some specified player (either the dealer or the player to dealer's left), and proceeding clockwise, each player states a number (talk about "halves" or "maybes" is permitted) of tricks. When the second player of each partnership bids, the final bid for that partnership is decided. A player who wanted to bid nil would do so at his or her turn to bid.

In round-the-table bidding, some people play that no one can bid 1 — so for example if the first player of a partnership says "x" tricks, the final contract must be either x, or else at least x+2. There is also a variation that concerns whether a bid of "zero" must be construed as a bid of nil.

In round-the-table bidding, some people allow a second round of bidding, in which each side may increase its bid. In this second round, the bidding proceeds exactly as in partnership bidding, beginning with the same side as the player who began the round-the-clock bidding sequence.

A variation found in any form of round-the-clock bidding is that no table talk is permitted.

SPECIAL ACTIONS/BIDS

There is great variety in the special bids or actions a player may be allowed to make during his turn to bid. Some of the possibilities are listed below.

MISDEAL

This may be called by any player whose hand satisfies certain conditions. The criteria for a misdeal differ — some possibilities are: 0 or

1 spade, 7-card or longer suit, no face cards. If a misdeal is called by any player, the cards are thrown in and a new hand is dealt by the same dealer.

Generally a misdeal may only be called before partner has disclosed any information about his hand, but some people play that partner may be consulted in the following limited manner. A player may ask: "Should I call a misdeal?" His partner may reply yes or no but may not disclose any other information about his hand. The reply is not binding.

NIL/BLIND NIL

These have already been described; nil is sometimes known as naught. They are sometimes valued at 100 and 200 points rather than 50 and 100. Sometimes the penalty for losing blind nil is only half the score for winning it (i.e. +100/-50 or +200/-100). If winning a blind nil is worth 200 then you are only allowed to bid it when your side is at least 200 points behind. Some play that when nil is played the bidder must exchange one card with partner; others do not allow passing of cards even in a blind nil. Another possible variation is that if you bid blind nil you pass one card to your partner and can specify one suit which you would like passed back; partner takes this into consideration when returning a card but is not forced to pass the suit you asked for. Some play that there is no penalty for sandbags when playing blind nil.

BLIND 6

This must be declared by a side before either partner looks at their cards. It scores 120 points if the side takes exactly 6 tricks. If they take some other number of tricks they lose 120. Some people play that to win blind 6 you just have to win *at least* 6 tricks. Some play that a lost blind 6 only loses 60, not 120. Higher blind bids may also be allowed — Blind 7 for 140, Blind 8 for 160 and so on. For some people Blind 7 is the minimum blind bid.

10-FOR-200

This scores 200 points if a side takes exactly 10 tricks, and loses 200 if they take any other number of tricks. Some people play that to win 10-for-200 you just have to win *at least* 10 tricks. Some play that any bid of 10 is automatically a 10-for-200 bid.

MOON OR BOSTON

This is a bid to take all 13 tricks and is worth 200 points. The side loses 200 points if they fail to take all the tricks. If playing with 10-for-200 the Moon or Boston is worth 500 points. Some people play that a successful Moon bid automatically wins the game (which is even better than 500 if you had a negative score).

BLIND MOON

This is a bid to take all 13 tricks, made before either partner has looked at their cards. It is worth 400 points if it succeeds, and the side loses 400 points if it fails.

NO TRUMP BIDS

These are not like no trump bids in Bridge, 500, etc. Spades are still trumps, but a player who bids some number of tricks with "no trump" promises not to win any tricks with spades, except when spades are led. You are only allowed to bid "No Trump" if you hold at least one spade in your hand. The value of the bid is double that of a normal bid for that number of tricks if won; the penalty if you lose is double the penalty for a normal bid (some people play with only a single penalty but this is not recommended). A bid of "No Trump" requires agreement from partner. The person who wants to bid "No Trump" ask partner: "Can you cover a no trump?", and partner replies "yes" or "no". A "No Trump" bid can be made blind, increasing its value to triple the basic amount. The minimum number of tricks which can be bid in "Blind No Trump" is usually set at one less than the required minimum number for a normal blind bid. A "Blind No Trump" bid is usually a desperation play and should only be allowed when the team is a long way behind — for example, more than 400 points behind in a 1000 point game. Failing in a Blind No Trump should cost the same as you win if you succeed — i.e. three times the basic value of the bid. However, some people play with only a double or single penalty.

DOUBLE NIL (TWIN NIL)

This is a bid in which both partners play Nil at once. One partner may suggest this and if the other agrees it is played. The score if successful is 500 points (or for some people an automatic win). If either partner wins a trick the bid fails. The penalty is variously set at 250, 500, or automatic loss.

In addition, if both partners win a trick, their opponents get a bonus of 100 points. A bid of Double Nil is only allowed for a team who are far behind — for example, more than 400 points behind in a 10,000 point game. In a few circles a "Blind Double Nil" bid is allowed. If successful, the bidders win the whole game; if not their opponents win the game. Some play that when a team bids Double Nil, each player of the simultaneously passes two cards face down to partner before the play starts.

BEMO

Bidding **Little Bemo** commits the team to win the first six tricks. It is additional to the normal bid; the team scores an extra bonus of 60 if successful and loses 60 if not. **Big Bemo** similarly commits the team that bids it to win the first nine tricks; they score a 90 point bonus if successful and lose 90 if not.

VARIATIONS IN THE PLAY OF THE CARDS

In the first trick, some allow a player who has no clubs to play a spade on the trick. In this case the trick is won by the highest spade if a spade is played. As the order of play to the trick may now be important (if you are going to play a spade, you would rather wait to see if someone else plays a higher spade first), the holder of the two of clubs should lead to the first trick (or the older of the lowest club in play if you are playing with jokers and the two of clubs was discarded).

Some play that the player to dealer's left leads to the first trick, and may lead any card except a spade. Some play that the dealer leads first and may lead any card except a spade.

Some play that spades may be led at any time — it is not necessary that they be broken first.

VARIATIONS IN THE SCORING

Tricks in excess of the contract (overtricks or sandbags) may be worth minus 1 point each rather than plus 1. In this case the penalty for accumulating 10 overtricks does not apply.

Some players use the units digit of the score to count sandbags but do not regard it as being part of the score — so sandbags are in effect worth nothing until you have 10 of them, when they cost you 100. In this variation if your score was 369 and you bid 7 tricks and took 9 your score would become 331 (not 341).

Some people play that there is a special card which cancels one sandbag on that hand for the side that takes it in their tricks. If the side which wins the special card makes no overtricks, or loses their bid, the special card has no effect. The special card may be either a fixed card — for example the three of spades — or may be determined afresh by cutting a card before each deal.

Some play that the penalty for taking fewer tricks than were bid is 10 points for each trick by which the team falls short of the bid, rather than 10 times the bid.

Some play that if a side's cumulative score is minus 500 or worse, that side loses the game (and of course the other side wins).

Some players set the target for winning the game at 1000 points rather than 500.

SOLO SPADES

In "rec.games.playing-cards", Meister (chrisor@l-link.net) mentioned a variation of Spades for four players without partners. Bids are for the number of tricks the individual player will make, and in the play, it is compulsory to beat the highest card so far played to the trick if you can; this includes playing a spade if you have no card of the suit led.

SPADES FOR SIX PLAYERS

This is played between three teams of two, partners sitting opposite (so there are two opponents from different teams separating you from your partner in each direction).

A 102 card deck is used, consisting of two standard 52 card decks mixed together with both twos of clubs removed.

The bidding and scoring are the same as in the 4 player game, and similar variations are possible. In the play, if two identical cards are played to the same trick, the second beats the first.

SPADES FOR THREE PLAYERS

There are no partnerships — players play for themselves.

THE CARDS

One standard 52 card pack is used. Deal 17 cards to each player. The remaining card is tossed out of play for that particular game.

Variation: play with a 54 card pack including big and little jokers as the top two trumps. Deal 18 cards to each player.

THE BETTING

Each player, starting with the player to dealer's left, names a number (called a *bet*). Each player's object is to win that number of tricks. Some people play that the total of the three bets cannot be 17 tricks — so that not everyone can make their bet exactly.

THE PLAY

The player who has the 2 of clubs must lead it to the first trick. In the rare occasion that the 2 of clubs is out of play, the player with the 3 of clubs must lead it. The other two players must play a club (not necessarily their lowest). A player who has no club may either:

Take it by playing any spade or —
Refuse it by playing any non-spade of a different suit.

The player who wins a trick leads the next. The other two players must play a card of the suit led, or if either player has none of that suit, take with a spade or refuse with a non-spade. If neither of the other players has a card of the suit led and both play a spade then the higher spade wins. A player may not lead a spade until a spade has been used to take another trick led by a non-spade. The exception is when a player has nothing left in hand but spades.

SCORING

Remember each player's bet!

If you win as many or more tricks than you bet, you gain 10 points for each trick bet. If you win fewer tricks than you bet, you lose 10 times the amount of tricks you bet (losing like this is usually referred to as a *cut*).

Sandbags are overtricks: If you take too many tricks, for every extra trick over what you bet, the amount you win for the contract is reduced by 10 points. For example, if you bet 4 tricks and take 5, you win only 30 instead of 40; if you take 7 tricks having bet 3 you lose 10 points over-all (30 minus 40).

Variation: Some players count sandbags. Instead of losing 10 points from your contract score for each sandbag, when you accumulate 10 sandbags (over several deals), you drop 100 points. This is why sometimes you will refuse a trick, since taking it will give you too many tricks, and you lose points.

The game is played to a set number, usually 300, 400, 500, or some other round number. When one (or more) pass that number, the player with the highest score wins.

VARIATION — BONUS SCORES

Szu Kay Wong recommends playing with the following bonus scores:

If you take the very last trick with a **high spade** (nine or above), and with that trick you make exactly what you bet, you gain an additional 10 point bonus. If you *bag* (get too many tricks), there is no bonus.

If you win an unbroken sequence of tricks at the end (2, 3, 4, or more tricks), all with high spades (9 or above), and get exactly what you bet, there is a similar bonus of 10 points per trick (for example, if you took the last 5 tricks with high spades to make your bet the bonus would be 50).

There is no bonus for winning the last tricks with non-spades or low spades. A bonus is not awarded to a player who "gets lucky" at the end by winning the last trick with a 4 of diamonds, for instance. On the other hand, if a player has the Ace of spades in his hand and waits until the end to play it, that is considered good play, and is rewarded.

For successful bids of seven or more, you get an extra 10 points for each trick bid above six. So if you make a seven trick bid exactly, you gain 80 points. Eight tricks exactly gains 100, 9 gains 120, and so on. This rewards those who are more daring.

Making a bet of exactly 2, 1, or none is also very difficult, and is rewarded as follows:

Anyone who bets 2 and gets 2 wins 40 points (instead of 20).

If you get 3, you still get 20 points (one bag). Four tricks is worth nothing, and every additional bag is -10 each (per usual).

Anyone who bets 1 and gets exactly 1 wins 60 points. If you get 2, you also get nothing, and each additional bag is again -10 each.

Anyone who bets none and gets it is entitled to 100 points. Otherwise, subtract 10 for every trick taken (just like regular bags).

Blind: You may decide to not look at your cards and just bet. This will double all points. For example, if you bet and win 5 tricks, you gain 1000 points. However, if you miss, the penalty is also double (in the 5 trick case, 100 points).

SPADES FOR TWO PLAYERS

There is no deal. Instead, the deck is placed face-down between the two players, and they take turns to draw cards.

At your turn you draw the top card, look at it (without showing to your opponent) and decide whether you want to keep it.

If you want to keep it you put it in your hand, and draw the next card, which you look at and must then discard face down;

If you decide not to keep the first card you discard it face down and then draw the next card, which you put in your hand.

It is then the other player's turn to draw. This continues until the stock is exhausted. You then each have a hand of 13 cards and have discarded 13 cards.

Now each player bids a number of tricks, and you play and score according to the same rules as for three or four players.

OTHER SPADES (www) SITES: (FOR FAST "LINKING" TO THESE SITES, GO TO JOHN MCLEOD'S HOME PAGE — http:// www.pagat.com/).

BIDDING

BIDDING IS THE MOST IMPORTANT PART OF THE GAME. NO MATTER HOW well you are able to play hands, the wrong bid can lead to a lot of problems. Each partnership strives to meet the **optimum contract**. The player to the immediate left of the dealer is designated as the first bidder, and then each of the other players bid in turn, clockwise. Unlike Bridge, there is only **one round** of bidding in the game of spades. This is why it is absolutely essential to listen closely to any bids which may precede yours — **especially your partner's bid.** In Spades, the only acceptable bids are the numbers 1 to 13, or a bid of zero which is called "nil" or "blind nil." ("Zero" is never actually bid, instead the word "nil" is used.) The basis of a bid is the number of tricks a player **expects** to take. For example if a player holds two Aces in side suits, and the King, Queen, and one small spade — a bid of three is quite reasonable. However, a bid of four is probably a bit aggressive in that the player may not be able to take two spade tricks unless his or her partner holds the Ace of spades. Another chance for an additional spade trick exists if the Ace of spades is held by the right-hand opponent. Suit names and the words "no trump" are never mentioned during the bidding and each player is allowed only **one bid per hand**. There is no call of "Pass" during the round of bidding: therefore, the minimum numerical bid is one or a bid of nil. It is quite possible that the total number of tricks bid may exceed 13. This situation would doom one of the partnerships to defeat. The fourth bid of each auction completes the round of bidding for that hand. Remember, the opening bid is made by the person to the left of the dealer.

EVALUATING YOUR HAND

In order to bid properly, you must be able to accurately assess the number of tricks you expect to take. Other factors which may influence your bidding are: (a) **the position of your turn to bid**; (b) **your partner's bid**, (c) **the opponents' bids**, and finally, (d) **the score at that time**. In Spades, you are rewarded with more points if you bid aggressively: however, if you are set or defeated — you stand to lose more than if you had bid less aggressively. Basically, the **higher** you bid, the **higher** the risk. It is important to understand the scoring situation at the time of your bid and the trick-taking potential of certain card combinations. It is interesting to note that the bidding system in Spades is geared toward the conservative approach. There is a spatial relationship of the math and the result of making and losing contracts. For example, at the beginning of the game, each side starts out with zero points. If your partnership has a combined bid of 70 and you are set, your score becomes minus 70 points. If you make your contract your score is plus 70 points. In other words, there is a **swing** of 140 points here. It is probably best to bid one trick lower if there is any doubt as to the possibility of making your contract. This applies to card combinations which are borderline or dubious. Hand evaluation and bidding techniques are reviewed in a later chapter. A great concern is the **duplication of values** in the same suit between you and your partner. The following card combinations are listed as a guide to help you gauge the value of your hand. It is reasonable to assume that an Ace will usually be worth one trick. Of course, the Ace of spades is a guaranteed winner. Aces in side suits will usually win tricks as well. However, the longer a suit is, the less likely an Ace, or for that measure, any high card, will win a trick. Kings are a very "iffy" proposition. If you hold a singleton King, the odds are very much against you. Either the opponents' Ace will drop your King, or your partner may prematurely play the Ace of that suit and swallow up your King. Thus, I rate a singleton King as somewhat limited and less than full value (though, as a face card, it does have some intrinsic qualities). The only instances where a singleton King has any worth (other than its distributional feature), occur when your partner holds the Ace or Queen of that suit, and does not play either card prematurely. Should you hold the King of a suit with two or three accompanying small cards, you have approximately a 50% chance of scoring your King if the opponents hold the Ace, and a much higher chance if your partner holds the Ace. If playing in a four-player individuals' game, the odds are greatly reduced. If your King is accompanied by more than three small cards, the chances of scoring a trick are greatly reduced. The only exception is the King of spades, which often becomes promoted when other high spades are played, or can be used to trump another suit. Queens are even more tenuous. A singleton queen is basically worthless and has value as any other low card singleton. A weak case can be argued for the use of a singleton Queen to help "cover" a nil bid, or to drive out an Ace or King. That is an example of stretching the limits. A Queen with one or two small spot cards is also shaky unless a partner holds the Ace or King. With the exception of the Queen of trump, the value of Queens in general, is speculative at best. Evaluating Jacks is a waste of time unless we are talking about the trump suit, and even then, the Jack requires at least two or three accompanying spot cards to be of any value. Even Queen-Jack sequences have a deflated quality — unless you have these cards in the trump suit. It is safe to conclude that **distribution** (singletons and voids) is of tremendous value. For if you are short in any suit, other than spades, you have the potential of "trumping in" for tricks when your short suit is led. The ideal holding is the singleton Ace of clubs, hearts or diamonds. Once you clear the Ace out of the way, you will be able to trump on the next lead of that suit.

Now we will cover what is called honor card combinations or **sequences** in the side suits (clubs, hearts, and diamonds). The accumulation of honor cards in the same suit greatly strengthens that suit. The Ace, King of the same suit will usually score two tricks unless there is great length in that suit. The King and Queen and one or two small cards in the same suit will score two tricks approximately 50 percent of the time unless your partner holds the Ace. Even then, it is a bit unrealistic to expect to take three tricks in the same suit, as the odds favor an opponent trumping on the third round. The Ace and Queen of the same suit will score two tricks 50 percent of the time with the help of a **finesse** (see chapter 13). Honor card combinations in the trump suit are valued much higher as their trick taking potential is greatly increased. Honor cards lose quite a bit of their potency if they are scattered among three or four suits.

PARTNER'S BID

Exactly fifty percent of the time, your partner's bid will precede yours. He will have the opening bid or the second bid and your evaluation of your hand will be affected by his bid. The higher your partner bids, the less likely some of your high cards will score tricks. This is due to that old "sea dog" — **duplication!** This is especially true in the side suits. The greatest fear in any contract is that you and your partner will have **wasted values** — that is, an accumulation of high cards in the same suit. Furthermore, if your partner bids a nil or a low level numerical bid such as one or two, your hand may actually decrease in value. (He will not be able to promote your middle cards.) It really depends on the **cards you actually hold.** Finally, it is useful to note that if either opponent bids a **nil**, you may be forced to take additional tricks, especially if you are trying to set the nil. The "covering" hand will sacrifice tricks in order to protect the partner's Nil bid. The ideal bidding seat is fourth position. In this case, you have the opportunity to listen to the other three bids preceding yours and then make your assessment of your hand accordingly.

BAGS (PURPOSE AND STRATEGY)

Bags, or sandbags, are a part of the game which affects scoring. The purpose of bags is to punish overly conservative bidders and to offset the occasional inequities of the luck of the deal. Without bags, the game is very dull and the bidding is very conservative. Each bag up to nine does not count as anything,* however, **an accumulation of 10 bags** results in a **penalty of 100 points.** The real strategy of the game is the balance between accumulating bags and making your bids. There are players who go blithely about their way, gathering bags as if they did not have a care in the world. After a few score reductions of one hundred points at a time, their partners become frustrated and usually resolve the matter. There is also a determination which needs to be made for the value of setting the

* A bonus of one point per bag is awarded

opponent's contract versus the number of bags required to accomplish this objective. We will cover this topic in greater detail later on in this book.

THE BID OF NIL

The bid of nil has a certain degree of risk. Unless you are fortunate to have a hand with all low cards and fewer than three small spades, you do have the threat of being set. The loss of 100 points is a very steep penalty for the defeated nil. The carnage is even worse for the set of a **blind nil** — a whopping 200 points! There are many fine players who effortlessly defeat many nils working cooperatively with their partner. The making of a nil bid is truly a **team** effort, as your partner will protect you — even at the risk of **losing** his or her bid! When you determine if a hand is worth bidding nil, the important thing to note is the **length and strength of your spade suit** as well as the number of unprotected high cards in your side suits. As for blind nil or double nil, this bid is best used when you are losing by a ton of points and must resort to desperation in order to have any hope of stealing a win. Anyone who makes an opening bid of blind nil for the first hand of a game should be marched off to the dunking tank, and immersed at least 20 times. The risk is just too great, and to start out a fresh game with a 200 point deficit is very unfair to your partner. Should you make a game-opening blind nil bid, you will incur the wrath of your opponents, who may very well counter with a blind nil bid of their own. Then the contest will be reduced to an exercise of nil bids, and random luck. For the record, a lot of players will not allow blind nil bids to be part of the rules. Remember, the bidder of a blind nil cannot look at his/her cards, and thus is at the mercy of the random luck factor.

BIDDING QUIZ

Here are twenty hands (and a bonus hand) for you to test your bidding skills. Please review each holding carefully and then consider the optimum bid. What is your bid for each of these hands? (The answers are listed after the last question).

A   YOU BID FIRST: DETERMINE YOUR OPENING "SALVO", AND GIVE EACH HAND YOUR BEST "SHOT"!

1. ♠ – Q J 3   ♥ – A K 8   ♦ – 10 9 7 3   ♣ – A 9 2
2. ♠ – 10 9 8 6   ♥ – Q 4 3 2   ♦ – 5   ♣ – K 9 8 6
3. ♠ – A K Q J 9 8   ♥ – K Q J   ♦ – VOID   ♣ – K Q 9 2
4. ♠ – 6 5 2   ♥ – A Q 9 6 3 2   ♦ – 7 3   ♣ – 8 4
5. ♠ – K 10 9 8   ♥ – K 7 3   ♦ – K 4 2   ♣ – K 7 3

B   YOU BID IN SECOND POSITION — YOUR RIGHT HAND OPPONENT HAS OPENED WITH A THREE BID. WHAT IS YOUR BID (FOR EACH HAND)?

6. ♠ – A Q 3   ♥ – J 10 9 5 4   ♦ – A 9 4 2   ♣ – 7
7. ♠ – VOID   ♥ – Q J 10 3   ♦ – K J 9 8 6 ♣ – Q 10 9 7

C   YOU ARE IN SECOND POSITION — YOUR RIGHT HAND OPPONENT HAS OPENED WITH A NIL BID. NOW IT IS YOUR TURN — WHAT IS YOUR BID FOR EACH HAND?

8   ♠ – Q J 10 2   ♥ – A Q 5   ♦ – K Q 6 4   ♣ – A K
9   ♠ – K 10 4   ♥ – J 7   ♦ – A 10 6 5 2 ♣ – J 6 2

D   YOU BID IN THIRD POSITION — YOUR PARTNER OPENS WITH A FOUR, THE RIGHT HAND OPPONENT BIDS TWO. GO AHEAD — PLACE YOUR BID FOR EACH HAND.

10 ♠ – K Q 3   ♥ – A 4 2   ♦ – 7 6 4 2   ♣ – 10 8 5
11 ♠ – 7 5 3   ♥ – Q 7 6 3 2   ♦ – J 7 2   ♣ – 8 4

E   YOU BID IN THIRD POSITION — YOUR PARTNER OPENS WITH A NIL, THE RIGHT HAND OPPONENT BIDS SIX. THINK CAREFULLY AND PLACE YOUR BID FOR EACH HAND.

12 ♠ – K J 10   ♥ – K Q 9   ♦ – A K 2   ♣ – Q 10 8 3

13 ♠ – 10 6 2   ♥ – 10 9 8 3   ♦ – J 8 7 4   ♣ – Q 7
14 ♠ – A K J 9   ♥ – VOID   ♦ – K Q 9 6   ♣ – Q J 10 6 4
15 ♠ – K   ♥ – A K Q 7 5 2   ♦ – Q J 4 3   ♣ – K 2

F   YOU BID IN FOURTH POSITION — THE LEFT OPPO-
NENT OPENS WITH FOUR, PARTNER BIDS FIVE AND
THE RIGHT HAND OPPONENT BIDS NIL. YOU HAVE
THE LAST BID FOR EACH HAND. MAKE YOUR SELEC-
TIONS.

16 ♠ – J 10 8 4   ♥ – K Q 9 2   ♦ – A K   ♣ – Q J 6
17 ♠ – VOID   ♥ – A K 8 7   ♦ – K Q 9 7 3   ♣ – A 8 6 5
18 ♠ – 7 3   ♥ – J 7 5 2   ♦ – A J 6 5 2   ♣ – J 3

G   YOU BID IN FOURTH POSITION — THE LEFT HAND
OPPONENT OPENS WITH FIVE, PARTNER BIDS NIL AND
THE RIGHT HAND OPPONENT ALSO BIDS FIVE. ONCE
AGAIN, YOU HAVE THE LAST BID FOR EACH HAND. GO
FOR IT!

19 ♠ – 3 2   ♥ – A 8 6 5 4 2   ♦ – Q 7 4   ♣ – Q 5
20 ♠ – A K 4 2   ♥ – K 7 6   ♦ – A Q 5   ♣ – 10 9 5

BONUS QUESTION — THIS HAND ACTUALLY
OCCURRED IN A TOURNAMENT. YOU HAVE THE OPEN-
ING BID. STEP UP TO THE PLATE AND TAKE A SWING AT
THIS "CURVE BALL"!

21 ♠ – J 10 9 7 6 5 2   ♥ – VOID   ♦ – VOID   ♣ – Q J 10 8 6 3

ANSWERS TO BIDDING QUIZ

1. Bid FOUR — This is very clear cut, as you have three expected top
tricks and a probable trump trick.

2. Bid TWO — A nil bid here is very suspect, especially with long middle spades and weak clubs.

3. Bid EIGHT — You have five sure trump tricks, two hearts and one club. With normal distribution, you could make an extra trick. A bid of nine is very greedy and not guaranteed. (Why throw away a sure 80 points in order to grab another 10 points?)

4. Bid NIL — The heart suit, despite its great length, is perfectly safe.

5. Bid FOUR — This is a brutal hand. It is reasonable to assume you will win two trumps and two of the side Kings. You may score three trumps if the Ace and another honor card appear on the same trick. If you have the opening lead, you will have to underlead one of the Kings. I would be inclined to bid three and hope that any extra tricks I took would be of help to my partner. An extra bag or two is acceptable in this situation. You may also be able to dump a winner if you have secured your bid.

6. Bid THREE — You should score two trumps (one via a club ruff or successful finesse) and the diamond Ace.

7. Bid ONE — A nil is out of the question with so many middle cards. This hand may get nailed for some baggage; however, can you really assume that the Queens will win tricks?

8. Bid SEVEN — You have an outside chance to score eight tricks. Why risk a sure 70 points.? Another factor is the possibility of sacrificing a later trick to take a shot at setting the nil.*

9. Bid TWO — There just isn't any more horsepower in this hand.

10. Bid TWO — You hope to score two trumps and the Ace of hearts, but you can't assume the spades are favorably positioned or that your partner holds the Ace of trump.

11. Bid NIL — If your partner cannot help you in diamonds, then it is just not your day.

12. Bid FOUR — Normally a five bid would be in order, but you must consider that you will be covering your partner's nil. You may have to

---

*The nil bid on the right is not favorable, as the high cards will be located in back of you.

sacrifice a diamond trick. The loss of your bid is picayune to the loss of your partner's nil. A four bid should make rather easily with this hand.

13. Bid ONE — Don't even consider nil! Two opposite nils are a luscious target for the enemy to attack. Your club suit is very weak; your spade ten could be attacked, and you cannot expect any help from your partner.

14. Bid (a safe) THREE — Count on two trump tricks and a diamond, or three trumps. If you were not protecting a nil, then a four bid would be reasonable.

15. Bid TWO — You hope to take a heart trick and a black King, but remember your first obligation is to "COVER" your partner.

16. Bid THREE — Beware of duplication in your partner's suits. When both players on the same team are fighting for tricks in the same suits, there is trouble in "River City"! There is little hope of setting the nil, and thus, you must settle for eighty points. Note — you have a "fair" chance of pulling down the enemy four bid.

17. Bid THREE — This is just about as much as you can expect opposite your partner's five bid. There is a slightly better chance to attack the nil bid, but ensuring your eighty points is a higher priority.

18. Bid NIL — If your partner is unable to overtake your Jack of clubs, it is time to try another card game. How about a nice game of Cribbage?

19. Bid ONE — Two opposite nils are a bad bet and there is no way that your partner can save you in either minor suit. You may even get set while helping your partner. Bid your one — if you are set, the loss of ten points to ensure a nil is a very good deal!

20. Bid THREE — You plan on sacrificing a trick or two in order to cover your partner.

21. (Bonus hand) — Bid FIVE — You have no way of predicting the number of trumps you will score, however a suit of this length should be worth at least four tricks. This is a very strange hand; a double void occurs approximately once every 12,000 deals. If your partner has as

little as the Ace of clubs and the Ace of spades, you have a chance to make ten or even eleven tricks. However, if your partner has nothing of value in the black suits and high cards in the red suits, his or her hand is worthless to you. Your length in trumps will enable you to lead the suit and perhaps, "crash" some of the honor cards together (on the same tricks). These types of hands are very difficult to evaluate. In Bridge, the holder of a long major suit and a highly distributional hand usually makes a pre-emptive bid at the three level. However, I would be willing to say that the best Bridge players would be hard-pressed to "scientifically" reach an optimal contract with this hand. In the game of Spades, we have just one bid, and it is best to use a more controlled and conservative approach.

MORE ON BIDDING — NUMERICAL (1–13) BIDS

PLEASE REVIEW THESE CARD COMBINATIONS AND NUMBERS OF *PROJECTED tricks*. "X" denotes a spot card (deuce through nine).Percentage probabilities in the game of Spades are NOT equivalent to those in the game of Bridge. Spades partnerships consist of two individuals participating as a "team." The partnership aspect of Bridge is much different, as there is a "dummy" hand, only one person (the "declarer") actually playing the hand for his side. However, there is a somewhat parallel comparison, and a lot of the standard mathematical tables for Bridge can be used a guideline. (Some of the percentages are identical). The numbers listed below are adjusted for Spades.

I. SIDE SUITS (HEARTS, DIAMONDS AND CLUBS).
    A. Aces (denoted by "A"),
        1. A (singleton) — one trick
        2. A x (doubleton) — one trick
        3. A x x (Ace third) — one trick
        4. A x x x (Ace fourth) **speculative** — will win one trick approximately 90% of the time. Remember, long suits have a risk factor!

5. A x x x x (Ace fifth or longer) **speculative** — will win one trick approximately 70 percent of the time, barring extreme length.

B. **Kings (denoted by "K").** Note: The location of the Ace is very critical with various King holdings.*

1. K (singleton) — **speculative** — should not win a trick unless partner holds the Ace or the opponents choose to duck.

2. K x (doubleton) — **speculative** — will win a trick approximately 50 percent of the time

3. K x x (King third) — **speculative** — will win a trick approximately 50 percent of the time

4. K x x x (King fourth) — **speculative** — will win a trick less than 40 percent of the time.

5. K x x x x (King fifth or longer) — **very speculative** and probably will not win a trick.

C. **Queens (denoted by "Q")** Note: The location of the Ace and/or King is very critical to Queen holdings.

1. Q (singleton) — **very speculative** — will probably not win a trick — partner must hold A K, and duck first round. (The opponents, however, may allow a singleton Queen to win a trick!)

2. Q x (doubleton) — **speculative** — will win a trick approximately 33 percent of the time.

3. Q x x (Queen third) — **speculative** — will win a trick approximately 40 percent of the time.

4. Q x x x and all other holdings — **very speculative** and probably will not win a trick.

D. **Ace-King combinations** Note: The trick taking power of Ace, King holdings is very dependent of length of partner's suit.

1. A-K (doubleton) — should win two tricks more than 98 percent of the time.

2. A-K x (third) — should win two tricks approximately 85 percent of the time.

---

*high cards accompanying the King will increase its value (KQ; KJ; K10)

3. A-K x x (fourth) should win two tricks approximately 50 percent of the time; and one trick approximately 90 percent of the time.

4. A-K x x x (fifth) — should win two tricks approximately 33 percent of the time; and one trick approximately 70 percent of the time.

5. A-K x x x x (or longer) — **speculative** — may win only one trick less than 25 percent of the time; two tricks is a longshot.

E. **Ace-Queen combinations** (Note: these are usually "finessing" situations)

1. A-Q (doubleton) — will win one trick more than 99 percent of the time and two tricks (depending on location of the King) 50 percent of the time.

2. A-Q x (third) — will win one trick more than 95 percent of the time and may win two tricks depending on location of the King.

3. A-Q x x (fourth) — will win one trick 90 percent of the time and may win two tricks depending on location of the King.

4. A-Q x x x — will win one trick 70 percent of the time and may win two tricks depending on location of the King; however the Ace should be taken on the first round. Note: The risk here is that the finesse will lose, and then the Ace will be ruffed on the second round.

5. A-Q x x x x (and longer) — will win one trick approximately 30 percent of the time; two tricks are virtually out of the question.

F. **King-Queen combinations**

1. K-Q (doubleton) — will win one trick more than 98 percent of the time and should win two tricks if partner holds the Ace and does not take it (an example of "duplication").

2. K-Q x (third) — will win one trick more than 80 percent of the time and may win two tricks depending on location of the Ace.

3.   K-Q x x (fourth) — will win one trick 70 percent of the time and probably will not take two tricks unless partner holds the Ace with fewer than two other cards of the same suit.

4.   K-Q x x x — will win one trick approximately 50 percent of the time, two tricks become **very speculative**.

5.   K-Q x x x x (and longer) — will win one trick approximately 25 percent of the time, two tricks are virtually out of the question.

G.   **King-Queen-Jack combinations**

1.   K-Q-J (three cards only) — will win one trick more than 95 percent of the time; two tricks approximately 70 percent of the time and three tricks only if partner has the Ace and does not take it initially. (Three tricks are a very remote probability).

2.   K-Q-J x (four cards only) — will win one trick approximately 90 percent of the time and may win two tricks approximately 50 percent of the time. Three tricks is out of the question unless there is a very unusual distribution of the suit.

3.   K-Q-J x x (or longer) — will win one trick approximately 66 percent of the time. Two or more tricks are very speculative with this combination.

II   DISTRIBUTION VALUES (SIDE SUITS)

Distributional features are essential to the evaluation of every hand.

1.   **Voids** are valuable as they provide the ability to trump or discard on the first round of a missing suit. This is often called first-round control.

2.   **Singletons** are useful as they allow the ability to trump or discard on the second round of the suit. A singleton Ace is golden and worth full value as one trick plus the clearing of that suit for second-round trumping.

3.   **Doubletons** in a suit are helpful, but somewhat limited. A doubleton Ace is quite nice, for it allows the clearing of a suit in two rounds. Other doubletons can

also be helpful especially when promoting trump tricks for partner.

4. **Three card holdings** in the same suit are virtually useless for distribution, as it is unrealistic to expect to win a ruff on the fourth round.

III THE TRUMP SUIT (SPADES)

Unlike side suits, high trumps are as good as money in the bank. For there is no way to trump a trump. Here is a list of the trick-taking potential of various spade combinations:

1. Ace (singleton) — one trick (Obviously!).
2. A x or A x x — one trick.
3. A x x x — one trick; possibly two tricks if partner has length or the spot card is high and promotes to a trick.
4. King (singleton) — **speculative** — if partner has Ace, you SHOULD win your King. If opponents have Ace, you MAY win the King.
5. K x or K x x — **speculative** — will win a trick approximately 50 percent of the time depending on location of the Ace.*
6. Queen (singleton) — **speculative** — will win a trick less than 25 percent of the time. Note: If partner has King, the Queen has value by driving out the opponent's Ace. She is also helpful if partner has the Ace-Jack combination, as the enemy King will be forced — setting up the Jack.
7. Q x or Q x x — **speculative** — will win a trick approximately 50 percent of the time depending on location and holder of the Ace –King.
8. Ace-King (doubleton) — two tricks!!
9. Ace-Queen (doubleton) — will win two tricks approximately 50 percent of the time depending on location of the King.
10. King-Queen (doubleton) — will win two tricks approximately 33 percent of the time depending on location of the Ace (Partner will have it one out of three times).

* If partner holds the Q-J-10, the value of the King is increased.

11. K-Q x or K-Q x x — will win two tricks approximately 50 percent of the time depending on location of the Ace.

12. A-J x or A-J x x — will win two tricks approximately 33 percent of the time depending on location of the King and/or Queen.

13. A-Q-J or A-Q-J x — will win 3 three tricks approximately 50 percent of the time depending on location of the King. The additional spot cards increase probability of the third trick.

14. K-Q-J — will win a guaranteed two tricks and a possible third trick if partner holds the Ace and at least three other spot cards.

15. Q-J-10 — will win one trick; two tricks if partner holds King.

16. Q-J x x — will win one trick approximately 70 percent of the time and two tricks if partner holds Ace or King.

17. J-10 x or J-10 x x — will win one trick approximately 50 percent of the time if the partner holds at least one higher honor card. Combinations such as these become very speculative based on lengths of suits in both hands.

18. Xxxxx (five spot cards) — should win at least one trick and possibly more if the suit if evenly divided. If you find yourself in a desperation nil bid with four or five small trumps, there may still be salvation — if you can UNDERRUFF spades played by the opponents (or partner).

Please note that all trump combinations are very dependent on the distribution and location of key cards in the Spades suit. Another critical factor is the sequence of plays by the opponents. The trump suit is always a premium feature of any hand.

DISTRIBUTION PROBABILITIES (NUMERICAL BIDS)

Many of the great Bridge players know that distribution (shape) of a hand is key factor regarding trick-making potential. If a hand is balanced, its ruffing power is reduced, and the need for more high cards is increased (in order to take additional tricks). On the other side of the coin, an unbalanced hand with a void of singleton, has an increased chance of winning tricks, especially if the holder has some trump length. Here is an interesting chart:

SHAPE OF YOUR HAND	ODDS AGAINST BEING DEALT
4–4–3–2	3.7 to 1
4–3–3–3	8.3 to 1
5–3–3–2	5.3 to 1
5–4–4–0	79 to 1
5–4–2–2	8.4 to 1
5–5–2–1	31.5 to 1
6–5–2–1	150.4 to 1
6–6–1–0	1384 to 1
7–3–2–1	52.2to 1
7–2–2–2	195 to 1
8–2–2–1	519 to 1
13–0–0–0 (Unique)*	158,753,389,898 to 1

Thus, you can see that balanced hands occur more frequently, and two suited hands are very rare. However, wildly distributional hands are lots of fun, and wreak havoc with any bidding system!

---

* Note: The odds of being dealt a perfect 13-card suit are so incredible! You would win the Lottery ten times in a row before you would have the opportunity to hold such a hand.

7

ILLUSTRATIVE HAND

THE TIME HAS COME TO DEMONSTRATE A TYPICAL HAND. IN THIS BOOK WE will follow these basic guidelines.

A.   The opening bid is made by the player to the immediate left of the dealer.

B.   The opening lead is made by the player to the immediate left of the dealer.

Let us look at this rather interesting hand:

ILLUSTRATIVE HAND #1 — "TEAMWORK"

NORTH
♠ K 10 9
♥ J 9 7 4 3
♦ 6 4
♣ 8 7 4

WEST
♠ J 8 7 4 3 2
♥ VOID
♦ K 8 5 2
♣ A 5 2

EAST
♠ VOID
♥ Q 10 8 6 5
♦ A Q J 3
♣ J 9 6 3

SOUTH (Dealer)
♠ A Q 6 5
♥ A K 2
♦ 10 9 7
♣ K Q 10

51

BIDDING

Score (First Hand) (0–0)

NOTE: ASSUME THAT THE LOWEST CARD IS PLAYED IF A SPECIFIC CARD IS NOT INDICATED.

WEST	NORTH	EAST	SOUTH
5	2	1	5

A quick review of the bidding is in order. West expected to take at least three trump tricks with a reasonable chance for a fourth trump as well. A sure bet was the Ace of clubs. There was also a good chance to score the King of diamonds. North expected two trump tricks, although this might have been a bit ambitious. East counted on the Ace of diamonds and might have been tempted to bid two; however, his partner's bid restrained him. South's bid of five was quite reasonable with three top tricks and the likely possibility of an additional trick in each black suit. If anything, his bid was on the conservative side, but he felt that seven was a very good contract. The combined bid of 13 tricks for both sides created an air of tension as the possibility of a set was quite high.

West opened with the Ace of clubs, as he was reluctant to underlead his diamond King. North played his four, as East dropped the three, and South heaved the ten. The club five went to South's King as North played the eight and East played the nine. The King of hearts was trotted out and South expressed shock at the appearance of West's deuce of spades. Another club by West was taken by South's Queen and the diamond ten was placed on the table. West played low and East was thrilled to win the free finesse with his Queen. East now grabbed the Ace of diamonds as his partner concealed a wry grin. It is usually a good idea to take an extra trick or two to help relieve pressure on your partner as long as you don't accumulate bags. Note — bags are not applicable here, as the trick total is thirteen. East finally led the Jack of diamonds as West played low and North ruffed with the spade ten. A low heart was covered by the six and the Ace and another small trump by West. West now led his diamond King, yielding a ruff-sluff. North discarded a heart as South trumped with his spade six. South now chose the spade five lead at this junction. West inserted the four and North finessed his nine (rather than rise with the King).

North next led the heart nine which fetched the ten and deuce of hearts and the spade eight from West. Finally West had to lead into South's Ace-Queen combination and the hand was claimed for the last two tricks. It's too bad that the Ace, King and Queen of spades clashed together on the final-two tricks, but that's the way the cards fell. This was a hard fought hand by both sides, as both teams scrambled home with their contracts. This is a good example of cooperative partnership play.

ILLUSTRATIVE HAND

ORDER OF TRICKS TAKEN

TRICK #	WEST	NORTH	EAST	SOUTH
1	♣ — A	♣ — 4	♣ — 3	♣ — 10
2	♣ — 5	♣ — 8	♣ — 9	♣ — K
3	♠ — 2*	♥ — 3	♥ — 5	♥ — K
4	♣ — 2	♣ — 7	♣ — 6	♣ — Q*
5	♦ — 2	♦ — 4	♦ — Q*	♦ — 10
6	♦ — 5	♦ — 6	♦ — A*	♦ — 7
7	♦ — 8	♠ — 10*	♦ — J	♦ — 9
8	♠ — 3*	♥ — 4	♥ — 6	♥ — A
9	♦ — K	♥ — 7	♦ — 3	♠ — 6 *
10	♠ — 4	♠ — 9*	♣ — J	♠ — 5
11	♠ — 8 *	♥ — 9	♥ — 10	♥ — 2
12	♠ — 7	♠ — K	♥ — 8	♠ — A *
13	♠ — J	♥ — J	♥ — Q	♠ — Q *

*DENOTES TRICK TAKEN

SUMMARY   (4)   (2)   (2)   (5)

TOTAL – 13 TRICKS   North/South – 7 tricks   East/West – 6 tricks

ILLUSTRATIVE HAND #2 — "BARGAIN BASEMENT"

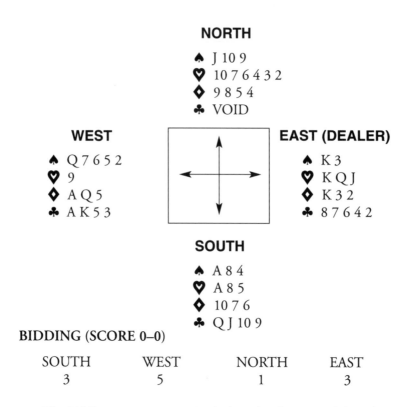

NORTH
♠ J 10 9
♥ 10 7 6 4 3 2
♦ 9 8 5 4
♣ VOID

WEST
♠ Q 7 6 5 2
♥ 9
♦ A Q 5
♣ A K 5 3

EAST (DEALER)
♠ K 3
♥ K Q J
♦ K 3 2
♣ 8 7 6 4 2

SOUTH
♠ A 8 4
♥ A 8 5
♦ 10 7 6
♣ Q J 10 9

BIDDING (SCORE 0–0)

SOUTH	WEST	NORTH	EAST
3	5	1	3

The bidding was routine. North thought about a Nil, but those two trump honors were a strong deterrent. East, South and North certainly brought their bidding shoes the dance! Thus, we had an inflated total of 12 tricks!

South "broke from the gate" with a nice lead of the club Queen, and West covered with the Ace. His eyes then rolled when he saw the spade ten from North's hand! North then led the deuce of hearts (a very lucky guess), as East played the Jack, and South inserted the Ace. The club Jack was covered by the King, (ducking would have been futile, as South had the finessing position) as North ruffed with the spade Jack. Now North played his last trump, and East played low, as South took his Ace. South then cashed his two good clubs, and brought his side's total to six tricks. It was the most economical six tricks you will ever see! Two Aces, two ruffs, and a nine and ten of a suit — pretty cheap stuff! That left seven tricks for the bad guys — and their bid contract was eight. These extra two bags were well worth the loss of eighty points for the enemy.

When East later complained about the opponents' good fortune and "off the wall" play, North simply stated "I would rather be lucky than good."

BICYCLE
8

EVALUATING YOUR HAND
(ANALYSIS AND REVIEW)

NOVICE PLAYERS ARE ALWAYS ADVISED TO REVIEW THE TRICK TAKING possibilities of their hands before proceeding with bidding. In the game of Bridge, we count losers in suit contracts and winners in "no trump" contracts. However, Spades has no dummy hand and two separate bids which are combined to produce a contract. Therefore, you are pretty much on your own. Logic and common sense are absolutely essential. As you become more experienced you will develop an appreciation for finer bidding techniques.

You have an advantage when you are bidding in third or fourth position, as the preceding bids provide you with information. First or second bids require a bit more effort to evaluate your hand. Many bidding techniques were reviewed previously. Let us now look at a rather instructive hand:

ILLUSTRATIVE HAND #3 — "BASICS"

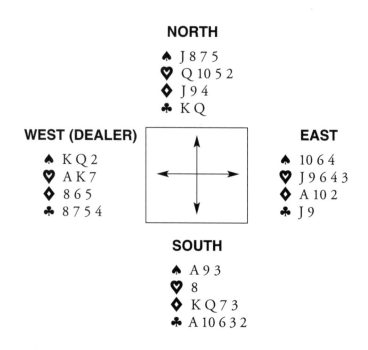

NORTH
♠ J 8 7 5
♥ Q 10 5 2
♦ J 9 4
♣ K Q

WEST (DEALER)
♠ K Q 2
♥ A K 7
♦ 8 6 5
♣ 8 7 5 4

EAST
♠ 10 6 4
♥ J 9 6 4 3
♦ A 10 2
♣ J 9

SOUTH
♠ A 9 3
♥ 8
♦ K Q 7 3
♣ A 10 6 3 2

BIDDING (SCORE 0–0)

NORTH	EAST	SOUTH	WEST
2	1	4	4

The bidding is a bit on the conservative side, for the most part.

North opens with a two, although many players would make a three bid here. East's bid of one is safe: however I would not argue if he tried a two. South is on target with his call of four. West has a decent four bid, but his balanced distribution and uncertainty about the location of trump Ace are a slight cause for concern.

    a.   If West was desperate for a four bid, he has an approximate 50 % chance of success.

    b.   East has a borderline two bid, but asking for a trump trick is very ambitious.

c. As for South, he has excellent hope for four tricks and even has reasonable play for five tricks.

The actual play of the hand is really immaterial; however, we will review it for instructional purposes.

North led the King of clubs as East played the Jack and South played the three.* North continued with the Queen of clubs and South once again played low. Thus, South was deprived of his Ace as the club suit was duplicated. It is generally bad advice to take away a short trick from partner. This may have the effect of setting up a free trick for the opponents and having your partner distrust you. Now, North shifted to the Jack of diamonds and East took his Ace with South and West following low. East continued with his diamond ten, and South immediately cashed the King and the Queen with everyone following. Now the eight of hearts was played as West rose with the Ace. The King of hearts was played and South trumped with his three of spades. Once again, a sure trick evaporated from someone's hand — in this case West's hand. South now played the Ace of clubs and North mistakenly ruffed low with the five as East scored an unexpected ten of spades. Another heart was played by East (a spade shift would have been better since it was known that South was trumping hearts); thus South scored another trump ruff. The Ace of Spades was now cashed and South exited with another small club as North ruffed with the Jack of spades. The spade eight was played and West scored his King and Queen. The rest of the hand was basically irrelevant as the bag count at that time was not a factor. Thus, everyone made their bid, although the play was a bit ragged.

---

* Note that small ("spot") cards in West's hand are immaterial.

ILLUSTRATIVE HAND #4 — "END PLAY"

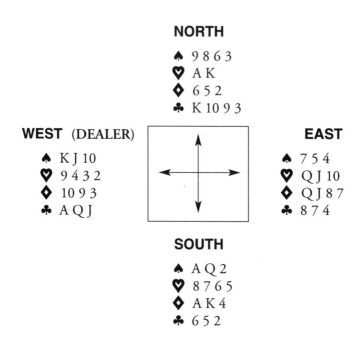

NORTH
♠ 9 8 6 3
♥ A K
♦ 6 5 2
♣ K 10 9 3

WEST (DEALER)
♠ K J 10
♥ 9 4 3 2
♦ 10 9 3
♣ A Q J

EAST
♠ 7 5 4
♥ Q J 10
♦ Q J 8 7
♣ 8 7 4

SOUTH
♠ A Q 2
♥ 8 7 6 5
♦ A K 4
♣ 6 5 2

BIDDING: (SCORE: E/W 474 – N/S 434)

NORTH	EAST	SOUTH	WEST
4	1	4	4

It was the end stage of a very difficult and long game. North trotted out a very optimistic bid of four. The King of clubs was very dubious at best. East contemplated a Nil bid, but those red suits were horrible! South's call of four was reasonable, with the primary flaw of a balanced hand. West's four bid was quite solid, with two very decent black suits.

Note the total of 13 tricks bid. If there are thirteen tricks in every hand, all bids, in theory should equal thirteen. In actual practice, this occurs relatively infrequently, as players tend to be slightly conservative. There is a natural fear of losing tricks in long suits, as well as finesses. Thus, the typical bid total is eleven. (This topic will be explored in a later chapter.)

It was quite clear that both sides were bidding aggressively in order to close out the game. The stage was set for one of the most brilliantly played hands in several months, and a truly wonderful ending! Expert Bridge players make this play effortlessly; in Spades, it is a joy to behold!

North opened with his heart Ace, and continued with the heart King, as everyone followed with their two lowest cards. Then he shifted to his lowest diamond (rather than make the awkward underlead of the King of clubs). South took the Ace, as everyone followed with low spots. Now South led his heart seven, and was quite pleased when his partner ruffed with the spade three. North led another diamond, and South was in with the King. A third diamond was played, and East was fortunate to win his Queen. (His one bid was done!) The club four was dropped on the table, as South played the six, and West tried the finesse with his Queen. North was thrilled to score the King! Phase one was complete. North had fulfilled his four bid! Now he set sail on helping his partner reach his objective of four tricks.

A neutral club shift was made in the forlorn hope of setting up a trick in his partner's hand. West grabbed his two club tricks, and bailed out with his last heart. Then he sat back, grabbed a beer, and waited for his two trump tricks to come home! As of this writing, he is still waiting! North trumped with the spade nine! Had he lazily played a low trump, East would have overruffed with the spade seven, and led a small spade through South — with very fatal results. Now the moment of truth had arrived. North played his spade eight, and East had to follow low. Disdaining the finesse of the Queen, South went for the sure thing — the end play! West was forced to win, and come right back to South's Ace-Queen. It just does not get any better! The net result was the fulfillment of the North/South contract, and the set of East/West. The game had been won!

9

THE BID OF NIL

BIDS OF NIL

A SUCCESSFUL NIL BID IS HANDSOMELY REWARDED, AND THERE ARE TIMES when nil bidding is the only hope to salvage a lost game. Most nil bids have a risk factor. Some are downright ludicrous! A supportive partner who can protect your nil is a great asset. No matter how you slice it and dice it — you still must have the cards! There are some nils which are quite solid, and others which fall into the borderline category. The time has come to review a few of the potential "underbellies" (weaknesses which can "croak" nils)!

High spade holdings can be very dangerous. Trump honor cards in your hand are the equivalent of icebergs in the northern Atlantic in April of 1912! If you hold the Ace of spades, (especially after a blind nil bid) — you are sailing on the Titanic! The spade King is also shaky and requires that your partner holds the Ace — a rather big order. The spade Queen or Jack are nuisances that can be alleviated by the presence of the Ace or King in your partner's hand or a very lucky lie of the cards — another ambitious request! Then again, there are those opponents who are very hasty with the play of high spades, which might allow you to dump a dangerous trump. Don't count on it in a game with seasoned opponents! Other explosive spade holdings are multiple high honor sequences such as K J x; Q 9 x, J 10 x x; Q J x, etc. Most of these will usually promote to one trump trick and can sink a lot of nil bids. Resourceful and clever opponents can also maneuver a player with a weak trump holding into a hopeless situation.

Holding of **middle spades** can also be very risky — unless you have two or less. For example: 10 9 8 or 10 x x x or J 9 x x can be a lot of trouble; however, 10 4 2 is good. Low spades are a premium unless you hold great length. Any four-card spade suit is suspect and a five "bagger" is big trouble as a "long spade" may promote to a trick. The only alternative with a long spade holding is to **underruff** (discard your spades under higher spades used in trumping). The greatest fear in holding trump of three- or four-card length while contemplating nil, is the risk of the opponents **cross ruffing** with their trump. This results in the establishing of a spade winner in your hand — especially if one of your trump is a Jack of Queen. I have seen instances where two small trumps in the nil bidder's hand were set up after the opponents took all of their trump separately — an extraordinary result!

To determine the soundness of a nil, you must evaluate the quality of your **side units** as well. Isolated high cards are a real problem and a concentration of high cards without accompanying low cards in the same suit is deadly. It reminds me of the game of Hearts in which the Queen of spades is the critical card. If you hold the dreaded Lady without sufficient "backers" or support cards, she will be drilled right out of your hand by repeated spade leads. Two or three key low cards (in the same suit of course) are usually safe, and a combination of low and high cards may also be quite acceptable. It often boils down to *which* low cards you may hold, the texture of the suits in question, and overall quality of your hand. Remember, it is not the high cards which are the threat, it is the **lack of low cards in the same suit** that can determine the outcome. Here is a guideline of combinations in the side suits which you may use to gauge the feasibility of a **nil bid.**

Please note that the next section of this chapter will review your partner's bid and that is often a deciding factor.

NIL BIDDING GUIDELINES —
CLUB, DIAMOND, AND HEART SUITS

COMBINATION (ONE SUIT)	EVALUATION
1. A Q 8	Very bad
2. A Q 8 5	Speculative/not recommended
3. A Q 8 5 2	Good
4. A Q 8 5 4 2	Fabulous!
5. K J 9	Very bad
6. K 9 3	Speculative and risky
7. K 9 5 3	Reasonable and worth a try
8. K 9 6 3 2	Marvelous!
9. K J 10	Horrible
10. Q J 10	Very bad/ asking for trouble
11. Q J 7 6	Speculative and risky
12. Q J 6 3	Borderline, but quite reasonable
13. Q J 6 4 2	Safe
14. J 10 9	Begging for trouble
15. J 9 5	Speculative — but close!
16. J 9 4 2	Safe
17. Singleton K	Off the wall — Do you expect your partner to have the Ace?
18. Singleton Q	Slightly better than the singleton King — and worth the risk in a losing situation
19. Singleton J	A reasonable bet especially if partner has bid 3 or more.
20. Singleton A	Give me a break!!!!!

Note — If you have more than ONE weak side suit, do not bid nil, Unless it is your only chance to salvage a lost game — or your partner has bid at least eight tricks!

Your opponents' bids are also a factor. If you are in fourth position and the opponents have a combined bid of eight tricks or more, a borderline nil hand becomes more attractive; however, if you have an obvious trump loser as well as a suspect side suit, you may be willing to reconsider your nil bid. Still, another outlet for getting rid of side suit losers is a void or singleton in another side suit. It is a bit thin, to be sure — but better than nothing. Another question that is quite obvious is: "are the opponents willing to scuttle their own contract in order to set your nil?"

In addition, they must consider the risk of accumulating bags in the process of attacking the nil. This is all dependent on the score at the time. If your opponents are bidding a total of less than five tricks, then you need much more overall quality (especially low cards) in order to bid nil. Finally your partner's bid (if you are in the fortunate position of having your partner bid **before** you) can quickly determine your chances of a successful nil. Remember, the higher your partner bids, the higher the probability that he will be able to protect your nil bid. If partner bids less than four, you realistically cannot expect help (covering), and your hand must stand on its own. A four or five bid from partner offers a modicum amount of support and a higher bid may be enough to send you on your way even with a shaky side suit. Never assume that partner can screen you from a potential losing card — just because he bid a three or four. Then again, most nils are mild to moderate gambles, and appeal to a Higher Authority may be the only alternative!

If you are contemplating nil and have the first bid, you are pretty much on your own. If you are bidding in second position and your right hand opponent opens with five or higher, your borderline nil bid now becomes more attractive. If you have the first bid of a hand, and your potential nil bid is very shaky, it is best to play it safe and bid a low number rather than risk a set on a high degree of speculation. This too, will be dependent on the score at the time.

BIDDING SUMMARY

1. **Distribution** is a critical factor in every hand. Voids and singletons (spot cards) are a plus.

2. A high bid by anyone (especially partner) tends to de-value your hand. Consider bidding one less trick unless your hand has a precise number of guaranteed tricks (usually in the trump suit).

3. **Protected honor cards** in the trump suit are important. Furthermore, **spade length** is a tremendous asset — especially if you are void in a side suit.

4. A sure bet is an Ace or protected King. In trump, they are "naturals." Good bets are **honor sequences** in the same suit (e.g., A K; K Q J; A Q J, etc.) Note: excessive length weakens the value of high cards.

5. Poor bets are: singleton high spades except for the Ace, scattered honor cards in different suits, and very long side suits. Do not over-value Queens and Jacks, as these cards are really hard pressed to win tricks.

6. Nils are sound bids if you have the **right card combinations** and **minimal trump risk**. A high bid by partner preceding your nil is very reassuring.

7. Your partner is your best friend — but you cannot assume that he will always have the key cards which you may need (for protecting your nil).

8. If your partner has bid a nil preceding your bid, and your hand has nil potential — **forget about it!** No matter how nice your hand, two opposite nils are a recipe for disaster! Remember, your partner may need you for your support of his nil.

9. A singleton or doubleton high trump, or a lengthy (4 or 5 card) trump suit is a strong deterrent to a nil bid. You cannot assume that your partner has the key cards to relieve you.

10. The use of the blind nil bid should be reserved for desperate situations (only). Never start a game with this bid. You must be losing by at least 150 points (or more) to consider a blind nil option.

ILLUSTRATIVE HAND #5 — "TWIN NILS"

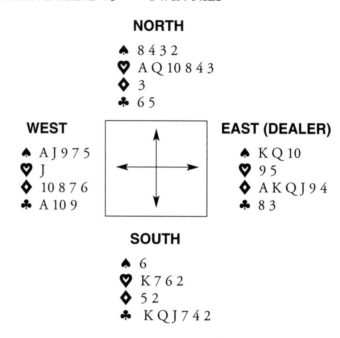

NORTH
♠ 8 4 3 2
♥ A Q 10 8 4 3
♦ 3
♣ 6 5

WEST
♠ A J 9 7 5
♥ J
♦ 10 8 7 6
♣ A 10 9

EAST (DEALER)
♠ K Q 10
♥ 9 5
♦ A K Q J 9 4
♣ 8 3

SOUTH
♠ 6
♥ K 7 6 2
♦ 5 2
♣ K Q J 7 4 2

BIDDING (SCORE E/W 333 – N/S 251)

SOUTH	WEST	NORTH	EAST
Nil	4	NIL(!!)	8 (!)

This is one of the most entertaining hands I have ever seen. It was played in the Ratings Room of the Zone. The score at the time was East/West 333 and North/South 251. Bags were really not a problem. Opposite or "twin" nils are quite infrequent and rarely made. Most players will not bid a nil after their partner has bid nil. There is no way to "cover" your partner's nil, if you make the same bid. Thus, you are both on your own, and the game becomes an "individual's" contest! In the meantime, the opponents are working together, and they immediately attack the twin nils by leading low cards of the side suits, and ducking whenever possible. The incentive for defeating both nils is quite powerful (a loss of 200 points for the opposition). Taking only one nil down is quite acceptable too — as the result is a "wash" (zero) for them — while you score whatever points you bid (provided you make your contract — of course!). You will really enjoy this hand, as the ebb and flow of the battle is what high-level Spades is all about!

The bidding was quite interesting, aside from the twin nils. West's four was normal, and East opted to "balance in" with an eight bid — partially based on the double nil, and partially based on his long diamond suit. It appeared that he was conceding the possibility that both nils might score, and taking 120 points as compensation would hold the net loss to 80 points! Then again, he did allow for an extra trick just in case one of the nils was set. The battle lines had been drawn! North's only concern was his 4-card trump suit. It was not the eight of spades that bothered him; it was the potential of having a trump established if the opponents got into a cross-ruffing pattern. A very daunting prospect was lack of ability to help his partner. I would suppose if you are up to your elbows in alligators, it is difficult to remind yourself that your initial objective was to drain the swamp!

South opened with his diamond five, and prayed that it would not pin a trick on his partner. West covered with the eight, as North dropped the lone three. East let go of the four — a rather dubious choice, but immaterial as the cards lay. West now tried the diamond six, as North ditched the six of clubs, and East forlornly played the nine — hoping to find the ten in South's hand. The discard of the two confirmed the futility of diamonds, as East shifted to the three of clubs — firing another salvo! South dumped the two, and West was in with the ten — (North tossed the five — his last club.)

It was deduced that the clubs were going nowhere, and hearts became the next suit of interest. The Jack of hearts was led, and North inserted the ten, as East dropped the nine, and South the seven. Now West played his diamond seven in an attempt to reach his partner's hand. North and South both pitched high hearts, as East took the diamond Ace. The five of hearts was a great try, but South alertly ducked with the two, and West unloaded his club Ace — hoping that North might be forced to take the trick. (A few of the kibitzers suggested that West should have played the spade Ace and tried to reduce his trump length with a cross-ruff. If West were playing with mirrors, that may have worked — his actual choice was very reasonable.) Alas — North played the four — and that plan went by the boards! A very frustrated East now started to run the diamond suit — in the desperate attempt to force either opponent to ruff with a long trump suit. North and South pitched their heart and club suits respectively and West was reduced to his five-card spade suit. On trick #9, he was forced to trump, and selected the Ace. This allowed North to unload his trump eight. It was of little consequence. The five of spades was the absolute last gasp, and North had an easy duck, as East was in with the King. The rest of the hand was routine, as East/West made all 13 tricks and North/South made their twin nils.

It was a hard-fought hand, worthy of praise for both sides. The true spirit of the game was on display. The game ended on the next hand, as North made an unbeatable nil opposite his partner's successful six bid.

ILLUSTRATIVE HAND #6 — "OFF THE WALL"

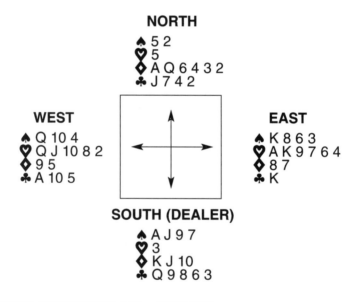

NORTH
♠ 5 2
♥ 5
♦ A Q 6 4 3 2
♣ J 7 4 2

WEST
♠ Q 10 4
♥ Q J 10 8 2
♦ 9 5
♣ A 10 5

EAST
♠ K 8 6 3
♥ A K 9 7 6 4
♦ 8 7
♣ K

SOUTH (DEALER)
♠ A J 9 7
♥ 3
♦ K J 10
♣ Q 9 8 6 3

BIDDING (SCORE N/S 364 – E/W 355)

WEST	NORTH	EAST	SOUTH
3	NIL	3	4

When the round of bidding was completed North was pleased with his partner's four bid, and made the comment "it has been one heck of a game everybody." This was a subtle form of "table talk" indicating to his partner that he felt quite confident about his nil. It is really hard to fault North's nil bid. After all, it looked like a lead pipe cinch. West started with the five of clubs, as North played the four, and East was in with King (South dropped the three). When the King held, East decided to probe the heart suit with the four. It was to be the "lead of the year"! Although South did not like his singleton, he felt that West probably had a middle or high heart or North had the deuce. However, West, who loved seeing the three from South, and in a display of serendipity, ducked with HIS deuce. The result was quite pleasing (and I am sure very appealing) when the five won the trick! North was absolutely shocked (an understatement) and immediately hurled several insults at his partner. Some of the comments included: "In case you forgot, partner, that was a nil I bid" and "I can't believe that the best heart you had was the three." This was followed by — "Why don't we just give them the game?" Finally a few choice profanities were uttered and the game abruptly ended.

Yes, it was quite incredible that North and South both held singleton low hearts and North's five was a winner. South with a nice collection of high cards in the other three suits was utterly unable to protect his partner. Certainly, this is an extreme example of duplication. Even though North later realized the unfortunate layout of the cards, his anger did not subside. He even went as far as suggesting that South trump the first round of hearts when the possibility of North taking the trick was apparent! (A revoke was a novel suggestion to be sure.) However, South had to follow suit and that was his crime. It suffices to say, that was the end of their partnership. The probabilities of two opposite singletons in the same suit occurring simultaneously are several hundred to one. When you consider that both singletons were very low cards, it made this deal almost unique.

BICYCLE
10

COVERING OR SUPPORTING
NILS — QUIZ

WE HAVE PREVIOUSLY DISCUSSED THE IMPORTANCE OF THE NIL BID. Because of the great bonus for fulfilling a nil, it is essential to ensure its success. On the other side of the coin, the defense will be attacking the nil at every opportunity. Often, success or failure will hinge on a critical decision. Here are some typical side (not trump) suit layouts. Partner (North) has bid nil, you are South and you have bid four. You hold in a typical side suit the various card combinations listed below.

I.   EAST (YOUR RHO) LEADS THE QUEEN OF THE SUIT
     IN QUESTION. WHICH CARD DO YOU PLAY WITH
     EACH OF THESE HOLDINGS:
     1.   A J 2
     2.   K J 10 9
     3.   A 8 3
     4.   K 2
     5.   A K 3 2

II. EAST LEADS THE SEVEN OF THE SUIT IN QUESTION.
     NOW, HOW DO YOU PLAY EACH OF THESE HOLD-
     INGS?
     1. A K J
     2. A Q 3
     3. K 10 9 2
     4. A 3 2
     5. J 10 6 5

III. FINALLY EAST PLAYS THE DEUCE OF THE SUIT IN
     QUESTION. WHAT IS YOUR CHOICE WITH EACH OF
     THESE HOLDINGS?
     1. A 5 3
     2. K Q 6
     3. K J 4
     4. A Q 10 8
     5. 10 4 3

IV. NOW LET US ASSUME THAT WEST (YOUR LHO) HAS
     THE LEAD AND YOU PLAY LAST. WEST LEADS THE
     TEN, PARTNER PLAYS THE NINE AND EAST PLAYS THE
     SEVEN. WHAT IS YOUR CHOICE WITH EACH OF
     THESE HOLDINGS?
     1. A 6 2
     2. K Q 8 6
     3. A Q 6
     4. K 3
     5. Q 9 2

V.   FINALLY, WEST LEADS THE FIVE, PARTNER PLAYS THE
     SIX AND EAST DROPS HIS KING. WHAT DO YOU PLAY
     WITH EACH OF THESE HOLDINGS?
     1. A Q 2
     2. A Q J 8
     3. A 4 2
     4. A 3
     5. Q 10 6

ANSWERS TO NIL COVERING QUIZ

(No comment means the play is standard or routine.)

I.

1. Play the deuce
2. Play the King (*Assume that partner does not hold the Ace.*)
3. Play the three
4. Play the deuce
5. Play the three (*This may cost a trick-a small price for protecting the nil.*)

II.

1. Play the Ace
2. Play the Queen (*Partner may have two or three middle cards.*)
3. Play the King
4. Play the deuce (*You must hope that partner has one card lower than the seven.*)
5. Play the Jack

III.

1. Play the Ace (*If you play low, your LHO may do the same, and possibly force partner to win the trick.*)
2. Play the Queen
3. Play the King
4. Play the Queen (*Try the finesse — it is virtually risk-free for partner.*)
5. Play the ten

IV.

1. Play the deuce
2. Play the King (*Observe the cards which were played.*)
3. Play the six
4. Play the three
5. Play the deuce

V.

1. Play the deuce (*Resist the temptation to take the Ace.*)
2. Play the Ace (*Continue with the Queen.*)

3.   Play the deuce
4.   Play the three (*Grabbing the King would be a very bad error.*)
5.   Play the six

Trump Holdings — Trumps are essential and very vital to supporting your partner. Remember, the most effective defense against a nil is the removal of trumps from the partner of the nil bidder. Once this is accomplished, the nil bidder cannot expect support from your partner via the ruffing of losing cards in weak side suits. Your high trumps are very valuable and must be played at the proper time. One of the most dangerous situations that can occur is the cross–ruffing of two suits by the defenders. As each enemy trump is scored separately, a three or four trump holding in the nil bidder's hand can become very problematic. It is assumed that a nil bidder will not try for nil with a losing high trump or five-card trump holding. Even a four-card trump suit consisting of all low cards is speculative. As for play of specific cards in the trump suit, the opponents' high cards can be ignored, whereas low or middle cards must be covered (unless the opponents are winning a sure trick). Remember, covering your partner's trump is very important and saving your key high trump can often make the difference in a close hand.

It is often helpful to save your trumps in order to ruff a weak side suit in your partner's hand. Basically, if you are on defense against a nil you must try to force a trump from the partner of the nil bidder. If you are covering your partner your objective is to protect or save your trump as long as possible.

Another very effective defense is the timed ruffing or "cutting" with high spades. If you are short in a side suit, and hold one or two high trump (A, K, Q, J), by all means, ruff with a high trump. This is especially true if your side's contract has been assured.

The idea is to promote middle or high trump in the Nil hand, and hinder the partner from "covering" the Nil. This maneuver must be precisely timed — otherwise the Nil bid may succeed with a weak trump and/or you may lose your bid as well.

The next hand will illustrate an absolutely perfect (and most ambitious) defense against an apparently ironclad nil. The timing of south was quite crisp, and he and his partner worked so harmoniously together. This is one great effort!

ILLUSTRATIVE HAND #7 — "RACE TO THE FINISH"

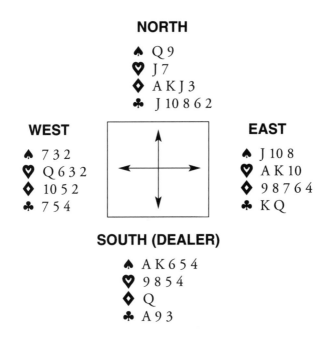

NORTH
♠ Q 9
♥ J 7
♦ A K J 3
♣ J 10 8 6 2

WEST
♠ 7 3 2
♥ Q 6 3 2
♦ 10 5 2
♣ 7 5 4

EAST
♠ J 10 8
♥ A K 10
♦ 9 8 7 6 4
♣ K Q

SOUTH (DEALER)
♠ A K 6 5 4
♥ 9 8 5 4
♦ Q
♣ A 9 3

BIDDING (SCORE: E/W 302 — N/S 282)

WEST	NORTH	EAST	SOUTH
Nil	2	4	5

A quick review of the bidding is in order. This hand actually occurred in a zone social game, not in a tournament. West's nil was very solid with only the slightest risk in the heart and club suits. North's two was a bit conservative but reasonable. East's four was quite appropriate and south had a reasonable five bid, especially considering the length of his trump suit.

West opened with the five of clubs, and North's Jack was covered by the King. South took the Ace and shifted to the singleton Queen of diamonds, beginning a campaign to remove trump from East's hand. The play was fast and furious and the hand became a miniature classic. West was relieved to unload his diamond ten and North flew with the Ace. He deduced that his partner wanted a diamond return and therefore continued with the King.

East followed with another low spot and South ruffed with a spade four — taking the trick from his bewildered partner. Next came the spade five, West played the three and North won with his Queen. Ignoring the diamond Jack, North switched to the club eight as he sensed the futility of the red suits. Whether this was a stroke of genius, a touch of serendipity, or just plain blind luck — we will never know. (North later said that West's play of the club five of trick one was an indication of a possibly weak suit.) East took the Queen of clubs as south followed with the nine and then he started on his high heart suit — a very good move. The Ace drew his partner's Queen, the King drew North's Jack and the ten cleared the suit as North eschewed ruffing. This was a most curious play as there was a reasonable chance to set East. Now East bailed a diamond and South ruffed with the six — his last low spade as North unloaded the Jack. The Ace-King of spades extracted two low trumps from both East and West as North pitched another diamond. Finally, the club three was placed on the table and West played the four as North ducked with the deuce. East showed out and down went the nil. North/South made their contract of seven; the nil was busted and East's successful four bid was little consolation here. It was a truly marvelous defense, a bit on the lucky side to be sure. However, I would be willing to say that very few North/South teams would ever set the West bid of nil. Perhaps someday I will place this hand in a duplicate board to see how many times the nil can be defeated!

ILLUSTRATIVE HAND #8 — "GOOD NIL — GREAT DEFENSE"

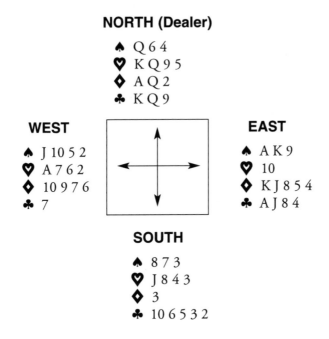

NORTH (Dealer)
- ♠ Q 6 4
- ♥ K Q 9 5
- ♦ A Q 2
- ♣ K Q 9

WEST
- ♠ J 10 5 2
- ♥ A 7 6 2
- ♦ 10 9 7 6
- ♣ 7

EAST
- ♠ A K 9
- ♥ 10
- ♦ K J 8 5 4
- ♣ A J 8 4

SOUTH
- ♠ 8 7 3
- ♥ J 8 4 3
- ♦ 3
- ♣ 10 6 5 3 2

BIDDING (SCORE 0–0)

EAST	SOUTH	WEST	NORTH
4	Nil	3	5

East made a very solid call of four, and South quickly bid Nil with his wonderful hand. West had a very comfortable three bid, and North, who was loaded with high cards, came in with a five. The Nil bid appeared to be very safe, especially with the singleton. But appearances are deceptive, as we will soon see!

East made the obvious lead of his stiff heart, as South played the eight, and West came in with the Ace (North playing low). The heart seven was returned (a club would have been better), and North split his honors (playing the King), as East ruffed with the nine. South was happy to unload the heart Jack. East now considered the casing of the Ace-King of trump, in order to remove protecting trump from the North hand. Instead, he chose to play on the club suit, and started with the Ace. South played his ten, and

West and North contributed their spot cards. Next came the club Jack, which West ruffed with the Jack of trump. Another heart was promptly played, as North followed with a low spot, and East ruffed with the Ace. Back came the club eight, and West trumped with his ten. Do you see the defensive unblocking pattern here?

West's last heart was ruffed with East's last trump, the King. The diamond King was trotted out, as South followed with his lone three. West played the ten, and North took the Ace. Now North began to worry about his five bid. On the other side of the world, South knew he was in trouble with those spade spot cards. North cashed the diamond Ace, as East and West played low, and South pitched low clubs. Another diamond went to East's Jack, as this position was reached:

NORTH

♠ Q 6 4

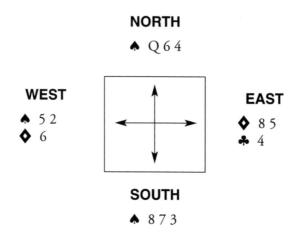

WEST

♠ 5 2
♦ 6

EAST

♦ 8 5
♣ 4

SOUTH

♠ 8 7 3

The diamond eight was led, and South now had the consolation of choosing his poison. If he ruffed low, then North would win the four. Now the Q-6 of trump just could not save the day! If South ruffed high, North is forced to win the trump Queen. The Master trump was overburdened. Sooner or later, South's spade seven would win a trick — and that spelled the end of the nil. And to add more injury to insult, North lost out on his five bid as well!

The opponents had contrived a very unusual defense which produced spectacular results! I suppose if you are going down for the count, let it be to brilliant defense instead of careless play or an unlucky lie of the cards. Well done East/West!

BICYCLE
11

BAGS AND THE
"RULE OF ELEVEN"

NOW WE COME TO THE SUBJECT OF BAGS. THIS RULE WAS ORIGINALLY ADDED to the game of Spades in the late 1950s. It has become the standard at most of the Internet sites and "live" events as well. There are a few players who believe that bags distort the game, however, they soon find out that this feature really helps to improve the game, otherwise the incentive to bid accurately is removed and players will not take a chance on reaching the proper contracts. Furthermore, there is no risk to set the opponents bids; thus there is a tendency to disregard overtricks (and bid conservatively).

There is a variation of Spades called "bag-em" — which is a reverse form of the game. The idea is to underbid your hand and intentionally sacrifice sure or expected tricks in order to force the opponent(s) to win unexpected middle or lower card tricks. Refusing to trump when possible, ducking when able to win, or underuffing are typical techniques. This approach can be very effective, especially if the opposition has more than six bags and/or is threatening to win the game. It is interesting to note that the "set" is the punishment for overbidding, and bagging is the penalty for underbidding. Advocates of the "bag-em" strategy just love to see eight, nine and ten bids!

While the idea is sound in certain scoring situations, it has the inherent flaw of throwing away ten points for each underbid trick. Some players go to extremes and embark on "bagging" opponents at the beginning of a game. The antidote to this is proper discarding, and trump management — which can "turn the tables" on the opponents — and dump the bags on them. Another alternative is to increase your bid by a trick or two if you suspect that the opponents are playing the "bag-em" game. In any case, you must be aware of the tendencies of your opposition, and react accordingly.

In theory, every round of bidding should add up to 13 tricks, and everyone should make their contract. It sure sounds logical! In actuality the typical bid total of each hand is usually 10 or 11 tricks. There is a reluctance to overbid your hand if you are penalized with points for a set or defeat of your contract. In spades, you are generally rewarded for being slightly conservative and punished for being overly aggressive. Let us now look at this layout:

ILLUSTRATIVE HAND #9 — "SAMPLE"

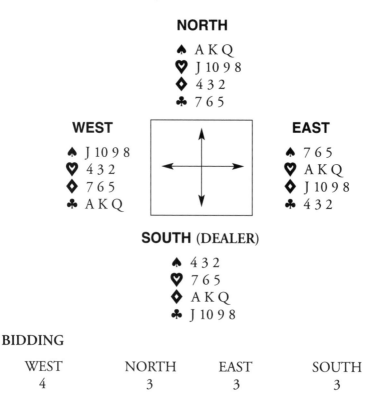

NORTH

♠ A K Q
♥ J 10 9 8
♦ 4 3 2
♣ 7 6 5

WEST

♠ J 10 9 8
♥ 4 3 2
♦ 7 6 5
♣ A K Q

EAST

♠ 7 6 5
♥ A K Q
♦ J 10 9 8
♣ 4 3 2

SOUTH (DEALER)

♠ 4 3 2
♥ 7 6 5
♦ A K Q
♣ J 10 9 8

BIDDING

WEST	NORTH	EAST	SOUTH
4	3	3	3

This is a hypothetical hand, which probably would never appear in real life; however, any hand is a possibility — including holding 13 of a suit. It illustrates the variables which can occur in bidding. Looking at all four hands and the bidding chart above, everything is quite accurate. Additional analysis, clearly shows that each player hopes to score their top three winners and the West player has an additional trump trick. As the cards lie, each player would make their respective bid. In reality however, the bidding would be a bit more conservative, as each player (excluding North) would not expect to score more than two tricks in their strong suit. Of course, a number of East and South players might try the three bid especially if they need the points. On the other hand, the North player knows that he has a sure three tricks, and the West player knows that he has a natural trump trick. The rest is a matter of judgment. In the typical competitive game, the East, South players would settle for two bids each, West would bid three and North would be three-thus yielding a total of 10 tricks. Now we will look at another interesting hand. It will show you how many a hand is often wrecked on the shoals of distribution.

ILLUSTRATIVE HAND #10 — "THE REEF"

NORTH
- ♠ A K 5
- ♥ 5 4 3 2
- ♦ 5 4 3 2
- ♣ 5 4

WEST
- ♠ 8 7 6
- ♥ VOID
- ♦ J 10 9 8 7 6
- ♣ K J 10 3

EAST (DEALER)
- ♠ 9 4 3 2
- ♥ J 10 9 8 7 6
- ♦ VOID
- ♣ A Q 9

SOUTH
- ♠ Q J 10
- ♥ A K Q
- ♦ A K Q
- ♣ 8 7 6 2

BIDDING (SCORE 0–0)

SOUTH	WEST	NORTH	EAST
7	2	2	2

Once again the bidding appears to be reasonable, albeit a bit on the aggressive side. South's bid of seven is very ambitious as he expects to score six tricks in his red suits, plus his natural trump. Another description of South's bid is that it is "off the wall"! West bids two, as nil is out of the question with a vulnerable club suit. In addition, West expects to trump a heart. North has an easy two bid with two top trump and a balanced hand. West has a safe two bid as well with a probable club winner and very likely heart ruff. (East bids a safe two) Furthermore the spade nine has a decent chance of scoring a trick anyway. With 13 tricks on the table, everyone seems to have the best of everything — fulfillment of their contract and possibility of setting the opponent's contract.

In actuality, the hand is a reef laden with shallows and submerged rocks. South leads the top of his heart suit and West ruffs away the Ace. Now the diamond Jack is played as East trumps and South helplessly follows. Back and forth they go! Six ruffs ensue and then East and West grab two top clubs scoring a tidy eight tricks. The last five tricks are conceded as the set is recorded. Note the duplication in the trump suit as the top honors are compressed between the North and South hands. It is unfortunate that South's beautiful hand was reduced to rubble, but that is the way the paste boards plopped.

The tolerance for bags is so critical that the score at the time really dictates the game plan. It is not worth taking four or five bags in order to set a low level contract. This is especially true early in the game. On the other hand (no pun intended), bags become irrelevant if the opponents are threatening to win the game if they make their contract. Of course, setting a nil results in a severe penalty to the opponents and is worthwhile — even at the cost of three or four bags.

ILLUSTRATIVE HAND #11 — "BAG CITY"

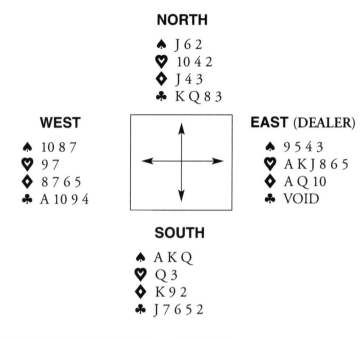

NORTH
- ♠ J 6 2
- ♥ 10 4 2
- ♦ J 4 3
- ♣ K Q 8 3

WEST
- ♠ 10 8 7
- ♥ 9 7
- ♦ 8 7 6 5
- ♣ A 10 9 4

EAST (DEALER)
- ♠ 9 5 4 3
- ♥ A K J 8 6 5
- ♦ A Q 10
- ♣ VOID

SOUTH
- ♠ A K Q
- ♥ Q 3
- ♦ K 9 2
- ♣ J 7 6 5 2

BIDDING (SCORE E/W 476 — N/S 436)

SOUTH	WEST	NORTH	EAST
3	1	1	2

The scores were close as East/West led North/South 476 to 436. It is also noteworthy that both sides had six bags each. East decided to bid conservatively upon hearing his partner's one bid as he felt that all they needed was three tricks to end the game. It was a very scientific analysis. What then followed was a lengthy dissertation by East regarding the mathematics and psychology of the game of Spades. He commented about he was an expert and prided himself on technique. Finally, he said to South, "This has been a great game, and you should not be ashamed of losing to us!" South led the club seven, and West played the four. North was in with the King. East immediately pounced on this with the nine of spades. Now everyone was treated to a discussion about the merits of reducing trump length in order to save bags, and how the use of the nine was such a "sweet" play. All soon heard this utterance: "I'd better make sure of our bid" and East promptly cashed the Ace-King of hearts (leaving North with the deuce). Next came the Ace of diamonds and assurance to his partner that an extra bag or two would be "peanuts." East's final comforting comment was "Don't worry, be happy — I have covered your one bid." He leaned back with a big grin on his face. North was careful to dump the Jack of diamonds on the first trick and South played the nine — a truly magnificent discard. Now East shifted to a small trump and South immediately cleared the suit by playing his three top winners. The King of diamonds was cashed and the deuce was placed on the table. East was buried alive with all good red cards as he easily reached 10 bags and dropped 100 points. The grin became an expression of absolute shock. It was a bad day for science! On the next hand North/South ended the game and East grumbled about how unlucky he was. These are the quirks which occasionally appear and you have to be prepared. East really played like a "drib" as he should have discarded the diamond ten on trick one, ruffed the expected club return (by his partner), and now taken his top red suit winners, as in the text. The diamond Queen is led, and South has no defense. If South grabbed the King, East would be out of the lead; if he ducked, East would have escaped with a low spade. (South has an interesting alternative by leading a club to his partner's hand.)

ILLUSTRATIVE HAND #12 — "THE OPTICAL ILLUSION"

NORTH (DEALER)

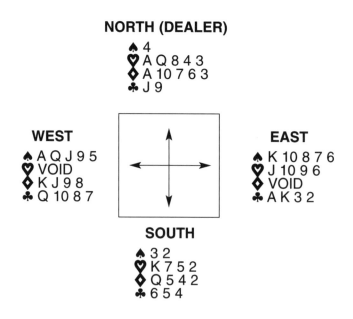

```
              NORTH (DEALER)
              ♠ 4
              ♥ A Q 8 4 3
              ♦ A 10 7 6 3
              ♣ J 9

WEST                              EAST
♠ A Q J 9 5                       ♠ K 10 8 7 6
♥ VOID                            ♥ J 10 9 6
♦ K J 9 8                         ♦ VOID
♣ Q 10 8 7                        ♣ A K 3 2

              SOUTH
              ♠ 3 2
              ♥ K 7 5 2
              ♦ Q 5 4 2
              ♣ 6 5 4
```

BIDDING (SCORE: N/S 355 — E/W 316)

EAST	SOUTH	WEST	NORTH
5	NIL	5	2

This is the most incredible deal you will ever see. It occurred in a tournament game on the Internet. I have never seen this happen! This is a hand which will probably appear once every 100 years. The bidding appears to be reasonable and South's nil looks quite solid. East led the three of clubs as he took an immediate shot at breaking the nil. South played the four, and West took the Queen. West now returned a club to East's Ace. East played the Jack of hearts, South played low and West trumped with the five. Now West played the eight of diamonds and North played the ten while East ruffed. North made the comment, "Oh my God," as he realized what was going on. East now returned another heart, South played the King and West ruffed with the nine, figuring North probably had the Ace. A diamond was returned as East trumped. Back and forth they went as they took eight ruffs SEPARATELY. West now cashed the Ace of spades, felling his partner's King. This left the deuce of spades as the only remaining spade. Amazingly enough, South was forced to take a trick with this lowly card. This was truly an incredible result. Surely it was a once in a lifetime occurrence. I wonder how many people could have possibly figured that South would lose his nil to the deuce of spades, especially considering all of the trump strength amassed in both opponent's hands. I guess it goes to show you that you never can tell what the Card Gods have in store for you.

BICYCLE
12

PLAY OF THE HAND AND DEFENSE

AFTER THE BIDDING IS COMPLETED, THE OPENING LEAD IS MADE AND THE hand begins. A complete review of leads will be made in a later chapter. The person to the right of the dealer commences play with a selection of the card which he deems to be the best possible choice. This can be a very critical decision, and the success of a contract is often hinged on the strength of an opening lead. Your objectives and order of priority in every hand are as follows:

a. **The fulfillment of your bid (making your contract)**

b. **The support of your partner's bid,** should that become necessary. This is especially true if protecting partner's **nil** bid.

c. **Setting the opponent's contract** (if possible) with minimal risk to yours.

d. The avoidance of **capturing excessive bags**. Watch those bags — they will kill you!

STANDARD NUMERICAL (NON-NIL) BIDS:

Assuming you have reached the optimal contract (and that is difficult to ascertain early in the hand), your immediate priority is **making your bid.** The bidding usually provides a reasonable amount of information, and will help you to develop "a game plan." If you have a good partner, he/she will take care of business from that side of the table! When you are on lead, a very logical choice is a solid suit headed by a sequence (e.g., A K Q, K Q J, Q J 10, etc.). A lead of a singleton "spot" card is also effective. However, if you are defending against an opponent's nil, your strategy needs to be adjusted. We will now review the play of standard (number) contracts. Try to avoid underleading Aces or Kings, as you may hand unexpected tricks to your opponents. This is fine if you are trying to escape bags towards the end of a hand; however, you must ensure fulfilling your contract **first.** A very good technique is the clearing of singletons or doubletons from your hand in order to pave the way for **ruffing.** The play of spades is usually delayed until the later stages of the hand. Sometimes the opponents will do the work for you and lead advantageously into your hand or allow you to make key discards.

If you have secured your bid, it is important to keep an eye on your partner's progress. It may be necessary to help your partner — even if you have to take an extra trick or two. It is considered good strategy to lead with your partner's short suit to enable him to trump early. Of course, setting the opponent (after guaranteeing your contract) is ideal. The higher the combined bid for both teams, the more attractive a set becomes. We will explore this further in the chapter referencing defense. Just for the record, it does not pay to grab a fistful of bags in order to set middle-and low-level bids. If you have a chance to discard losers in order to avoid bags, it is best to unload unprotected middle cards. Another fine tactic is to reduce or shorten the length of a suit by making strategic discards on the suit in play. There are many situations where this is a much better choice than the use of a trump. It could allow you to score a needed ruff. Finally, if your right hand opponent leads a low card, a good rule of thumb is to play a low card as well (referred to as **second hand low**). There are a few exceptions and those are based on situations at the time. This allows the partner a chance to win the trick.

Don't grab Aces too quickly! Give your partner a chance to win a King or Queen in the fourth position. Nothing is more frustrating than to "fly" with an Ace prematurely and swallow up your partner's King or Queen. Another trusty rule of thumb is **third hand high**. If two small cards are played preceding your turn, you should play your highest card in third position unless you are trying to avoid a bag. Otherwise, the last player will win a trick cheaply (with a low or middle card).

Sometimes, you will find yourself in a bit of trouble during the play of the hand. It is always better to take an extra trick that you were probably going to win anyway to allow partner an additional option. Observe very closely the cards with which your partner leads and discards. If he is dumping high cards, it is probably a bag avoidance maneuver. It is generally considered very bad technique to take a trick away from your partner unless you have a very good reason for doing so (e.g., returning a suit for your partner to ruff). In most contracts, you must determine your sure winners first, and then try to develop tricks in those suits which are missing key honor cards. I cannot overemphasize the importance of controlling bags. It is useless to make contracts with overtricks on a regular basis. If this is occurring frequently, you and your partner need to have a discussion regarding your bidding styles.

ILLUSTRATIVE HAND #13 — "TRUMP MANAGEMENT"

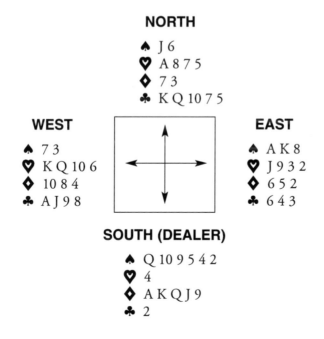

NORTH
♠ J 6
♥ A 8 7 5
♦ 7 3
♣ K Q 10 7 5

WEST
♠ 7 3
♥ K Q 10 6
♦ 10 8 4
♣ A J 9 8

EAST
♠ A K 8
♥ J 9 3 2
♦ 6 5 2
♣ 6 4 3

SOUTH (DEALER)
♠ Q 10 9 5 4 2
♥ 4
♦ A K Q J 9
♣ 2

BIDDING (SCORE: N/S 305 — E/W 294)

WEST	NORTH	EAST	SOUTH
2	2	2	7 (!)

In the qualifying Rounds of a Tournament, this is the eighth hand of a game. West, North, and East have somewhat reasonable two bids — although the West bid is a bit ambitious. North is also an optimist — as he is expecting a club trick! There is a lot of "heavy" bidding here! South makes a very aggressive call of seven. This is much too greedy, as the trump suit is quite ragged, and may not "break" (distribute) normally. A six bid is far safer — even if a bag is gathered. It just does not make sense to risk a contract of eight tricks for an extra ten points — especially at the start of a game.

The South plan is quite simple — flush out the enemy trump, and run the diamonds. It sounds good, and requires good technique and a bit of luck. He also happens to be an expert player, and sometimes you can take chances if you have good "declarer" (play of the hand) experience. The analogy to Bridge is quite appropriate here, as the South hand is the controlling factor of this deal.

West opens with the diamond ten, a neutral choice. South takes the Jack — a signal to all that his suit is solid. It is essential for South to utilize his trump suit, and he thus shifts to his singleton heart. West plays his King, and North covers with the Ace as East plays low. North now leads the King of clubs (a very good play), and West grabs the Ace. If West plays a heart or club, South's path is easier — but there is no way he will continue with a diamond, especially knowing the strength of that suit in the opponent's hand! Besides, the heart Queen looks like a winner — and so the choice of the high heart is made. This is ruffed with the deuce by South, and the first of the crossroads is reached.

The trump four is led. His partner probably does not hold the Ace or King (he bid only two). Is the Jack too much to ask for? Luckily, partner produces the Jack which forces the Ace. Now South can win any return, and drive out the spade King — which clears the path for extracting the remaining trump and cashing of the long diamond suit. (Yes, yes, I know that if East had the A K J of trump, South would be in deep trouble — but East bid only two!)

Continuing the actual play, East returns a heart, and South ruffs with the five. Now the trump nine is lead, and East in with the King. Another heart (by East) is ruffed with the ten, and spade Queen pulls the last trump — and it's diamond city!

South thus scores five diamond tricks and four trump. North scores his heart Ace, and the ten tricks result in set of East-West, and a very nice start for North-South. Regardless of the result, I still stand by my recommendation of a six bid for South. However, it is difficult to argue with success, and the south player backed up his bid with some really nice plays!

NILS (COVERING)

Protecting your partner's nil bid is a key element of the game. This is referred to as "**covering a nil.**" Just because your partner bids nil, does not mean that it is ironclad. As a matter of fact, most nils have a weakness which I jokingly refer to as the "underbelly." Basically, it is a race between you and the defense. It does remind me a bit of the battles which occur in the game of bridge when no-trump contracts are in play! You are trying to protect potential weaknesses in your partner's hand and the defense is trying to force your partner to win a trick. The point value of a nil is just too great to ignore. This example will give you an understanding of just what is at stake. Suppose the score in a close game is tied — you and your opponents have 300 points each — your partner has bid nil, you have bid five, the opponents have bid six. If you fulfill your nil as well as your bid, you will reach 450 points. If your partner's nil is set and you make your bid, you will lose 50 points. An absolute disaster is to lose the nil and your bid, which leaves you at 150 points. Thus, you can see the "swing" value of points for a nil is really 200 — the difference between making the nil and going set. You must go all out to protect or cover your partner — even at the cost of losing your bid. There is only one exception, and that is the setting of the opponent's **high level bid** and the fulfillment of your own contract. For example: if the opponents have bid 10 or 11 tricks and your partner has bid nil, and you have the opportunity to set the opponents contract — by all means go for it! The result will be a deduction of 100 or 110 points from your opponents' score even if your partner loses his/her nil. Although this is a "wash" (trade-off) or sorts, it is important to deprive the "enemy" of such large gains. Basically, it depends once again, on the score at the time, especially if the opponents are approaching game. Often, you will see the opponents conceding your nil if the difference is advantageous to them.

When you are playing opposite your partner's nil, you should try to get the lead; however, if an opponent plays a high card, the best strategy is to allow that card to win. If you hold the K 9 8 of clubs and an opponent plays the Queen of clubs, grabbing the King could be an error since you may need to sacrifice it in order to protect your partner. If the Ace does not appear after two rounds of clubs you may deduce that partner probably holds it and wants you to shift suits. A solid side suit of your own may allow partner to make discards. For example: if you hold A Q 9 8 5 of diamonds., your best play is to lead the Ace. Should your partner hold the King, he will drop it under the Ace and you should continue with the Queen. This will allow your partner to get rid of another middle diamond. Hopefully, he will not hold the K J 10 of this suit without a low card; otherwise you may question his nil bid! Your partner becoming void in a suit presents an ideal situation for support. Simply lead any card; preferably highest in your partner's void suit — that will enable him/her to make more discards of dangerous cards, especially Aces. If trumps have been "broken," then lead your highest spades. You must assume that your partner did not bid nil with a natural trump trick. Some experienced players prefer to save a trump or two — in the event it becomes necessary to ruff a possible losing card in a partner's weak side suit. And now for some "no-no's" regarding the protection of a nil bid:

a. **Never lead a low card!*** It is the "kiss of death" for a nil and your partner will not be a happy camper. The lead of a low card will probably be followed by a low card by your left hand opponent, and your partner may be forced to win a chintzy middle card trick.

b. **Do not lead middle cards of a suit if you have higher cards in the same suit.** This may force an honor card from your partner's hand.

c. **Do not overtake a high card played by an opponent.** For example: If you hold the Ace of clubs, and the opponent leads the K or Q, save your Ace for later. Your partner may need it to discard a middle club.

* unless your partner is void in that suit!

d. **Never lead a middle or low trump** (especially if you hold the Ace or King). Your partner may get "skewered" with a ten, Jack, or Queen.

e. **Do not overruff the opponents play of a spade on a side suit.** Save your middle or high spades for the end of the hand.

PLAYING A NIL

If you have a steady, dependable partner, half of your battle is over. Nothing instills more confidence than knowing that when the going gets tough, your partner is there for you. Assess your hand for any potential weaknesses. Sometimes you may need to take a chance and play a middle or high card early in hope of help from your partner. For example. If you have a balanced hand and you hold the 10 and 2 of hearts your best play is the 10 of hearts, even is this is an opening lead. Unless your partner has bid one or two, it is very reasonable to assume that he has at least the Jack of hearts. The odds of the opponents holding all four heart honors are less than 5 percent. However. If you are void in a suit, or hold a singleton, you may try to obtain a heart discard. Lead with your singleton or a safe side suit and try to give the lead to your partner for a favorable return. If possible, save critical low cards of the same suit for the end of a hand. Remember, long suits with lots of low cards are usually safe. There is no need to discard any cards from these suits. Instead try to discard dangerous middle or high cards of other suits. If trumps have been broken, underruffing a trump trick is generally a good idea, so long as your remaining trump or trumps are not vulnerable. Finally, counting suits and remembering spot cards is a real plus. There are just too many players who "fly by the seat of their pants" or play by "instinct." If you place too much reliance on random luck, then sooner or later you will be burned. When playing nils, make the effort to track honor cards and the number of cards played in your critical suits. Nothing is more frustrating than to make the wrong discard at the end of the hand and be forced to win the last trick with a card you could have unloaded earlier. It's just worth it to make the effort and earn the reward.

PLAY OF THE HAND — REVIEW

Here are some interesting hands. Note: The terms "LHO" (Left Hand Opponent) and "RhO" (Right Hand Opponent") are used. Secondly, the opening leads have been varied (for these hands only) in order to provide for some in-depth analysis. Finally, the plays are based on reasonably normal distribution of all suits.

HAND 1. Your LHO bids two; Partner bids four; RHO bids two; and you bid four. The opening lead is the Jack of diamonds from your RHO. You hold:

♠ K 10 5   ♥ A K 4   ♦ Q 3 2   ♣ A J 10 2

Cover with the Queen of diamonds, as you want to shed this card early. (It may also help to promote the King for your partner.) If your LHO wins this trick, you will be in good shape if he shifts to a club. This will allow for later options depending on which club appears on the first round. When you get the lead, play the Ace of hearts, followed by the King. If both of these win, then continue with the heart four. You should be able to score a trump trick, as well as the Ace of clubs, making four. If a high heart is ruffed on the second round, you need to try for two spade tricks or two club tricks. Perhaps your partner will be able to help you here. The opponents will be gunning for you, as you have an eight bid on the table, and they can take a few bags in exchange for a set! If the Ace of hearts is ruffed on the first round, then call in the dogs and give up the hunt!

HAND 2. Your partner opens the round of bidding with a nil; RHO bids five; you bid three (your normal bid would be four), and the LHO bids three. The LHO leads with the Queen of hearts, your partner plays the nine. You hold:

♠ J 10 2   ♥ A 10 6   ♦ A Q 4   ♣ K Q 8

Assuming that your RHO plays low, duck the Queen of hearts with the six. Save your Ace of hearts for later protection. Your partner may have another middle dangerous heart. If LHO now shifts to a club, duck this as well, unless your partner is winning the trick with a middle card. When heart is led, step up with the Ace and cash the ten of hearts. (If your partner held the heart Jack, it would have been discarded on the Queen, and if he held the heart King, it would have gone under the Ace.) Thus the ten is clean! Resist the lure of the diamond suit, and play the

King of clubs. A lot of scenarios depend on leads by defenders. Finally, if your partner produces the Ace of clubs or a spade honor (and either wins a trick), pretend that you have an upset stomach and ask to be excused from the table.

HAND 3. You bid five, LHO bids four, your partner bids one, and RHO bids two. The opening lead is the four of diamonds by your RHO. You hold:

♠ A K 8 4   ♥ K 7 2   ♦ A K 2   ♣ Q J 3

You have four top tricks in spades and diamonds. In order to fulfill your ambitious bid of five, you must hope to win the King of hearts, a club honor or a long trump. I would have bid four with this hand; however, we are in for five and that's the way it is. Take the Ace-King of diamonds, followed by the two; maybe your partner will be able to ruff the third round. If a heart is now led and the Ace appears, you have your fifth trick. If the Ace does not appear, then you must play the King and hope that the Ace is in a favorable position. If the heart suit does not behave for you, then you are reduced to desperation and must hope that you can score a club honor. The opponents are clearly marked with the high spades, and the Queen-Jack of trump are probably positioned in back of your Ace-King and two spot cards. Then again, your partner may realize your plight and perhaps take an extra trick for you.

HAND 4. Your partner bids three; RHO bids three; you bid four; and your LHO bids three. You hold:

♠ K 9 5 3   ♥ 4   ♦ K Q 6 4   ♣ A 5 3 2

This is a "pattern" hand. Once again, your bid is somewhat aggressive but considering the distribution it is reasonable. One thing is for sure — the total of tricks is thirteen, and both sides need to be on their toes! You hope to use your low spades for ruffs in the heart suit.

The opening lead is the Queen of clubs from the LHO. Your partner plays low (probably denying the King), and you hop up with the Ace. Now, you play your low heart. Surely, he has an honor card in hearts or an entry in diamonds, which will provide the impetus for a heart return. **As in Bridge or Whist, it is usually a good idea to return your partner's first led suit. However, consider the overall situation before making this "automatic" play.**

The plan is to ruff two hearts and win a guaranteed four tricks. The alternative is to ruff one heart and take the spade King later. You are already assured of a trick in each minor suit barring unusual distribution. If your partner has a solid three bid, you have a good chance of setting the opponents as well.

HAND 5. Your partner bids four; RHO bids three; you bid six, and LHO bids a very predictable nil. The opening lead from your right hand opponent is the Ace of diamonds. You hold:

♠ A K 10 9 8 3   ♥ K Q J 10 4   ♦ VOID   ♣ A7

Your bid is quite reasonable especially considering the strength of your spade suit. Once again, thirteen tricks are on the table. This seemingly simple hand is quite complicated, and full of multiple variations. Setting the nil is a very remote possibility — you must try to make your bid, and hold the loss of points to 30 (for the hand). Another plan now hatches. The nil bidder is on your **left**, and will not be able to attack your bid (or take defensive tricks)! Nailing his partner's three bid will give you a small profit for the hand! Ruff the diamond lead with the spade three, and immediately lead the spade ten. (An alternative choice is to discard the seven of clubs on the first trick which allows for later ruffing possibilities in the club suit.) Your lead of the ten of spades may let your partner score the Queen or play the Jack and force the Queen out. It's okay even if your partner has only two spot cards in trump., as long as the LHO followed to the first round. The ten loses to a spade honor on the right, and you are still in good shape. Partner will be able to lead a spade for a finesse through the other spade honor (on the right). If a high diamond is returned at this point, ruff it low and force out the heart Ace. A club lead is stronger — rather than allow us to score all of our trump individually. We take the club Ace, and shift to the heart TEN! This will make your partner play the Ace if he has it. Now a spade return by your partner is deadly! But the worst case scenario now happens! Let's assume that our RHO holds the heart Ace. My goodness, what did your partner have for his four bid? Our very capable RHO now continues with the King of diamonds — the best defense. We ruff with the nine of trump. Now, we play the Ace-King of spades. If distributions are normal, the remaining honor will fall. Once again the worst happens! The Queen of spades does not drop, as our RHO held four spades. We ignore the Master Trump which is outstanding in the enemy hand and proceed to cash out the heart suit. The RHO can take his spade Queen whenever he likes, and we limit the loss to two trump and the heart Ace. (I know, some of you may ask, "How about the King of clubs?") Well, I suppose that our friendly RHO could have THIS card as well. In that case, the whole hand was hopelessly "stacked," and your partner should have bid nil as well! The play of the hand in Spades is very comparable to the play of the hand in Bridge. An expert player at the helm will bring in many contracts and work cooperatively with partner to set opponents' bids. Practice is the best way to "hone" your skills.

ILLUSTRATIVE HAND #14 — "PROTECTING THE NIL"

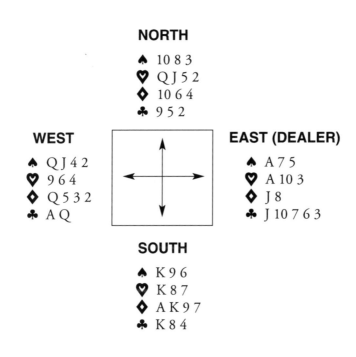

NORTH
♠ 10 8 3
♥ Q J 5 2
♦ 10 6 4
♣ 9 5 2

WEST
♠ Q J 4 2
♥ 9 6 4
♦ Q 5 3 2
♣ A Q

EAST (DEALER)
♠ A 7 5
♥ A 10 3
♦ J 8
♣ J 10 7 6 3

SOUTH
♠ K 9 6
♥ K 8 7
♦ A K 9 7
♣ K 8 4

BIDDING (SCORE: E/W 255 – N/S 153)

SOUTH	WEST	NORTH	EAST
4	4	NIL	3

South's bid of 4 was quite acceptable despite his three unsupported Kings — after all — his partner may have an Ace or two. West was really stretching with his "Queensie" hand. North's nil was a bit suspect; however, the score dictated an aggressive move, and the four bid by his partner was somewhat reassuring. East's bid was normal.

South, on lead, now had a devalued hand, and his objective was to protect his partner's nil — even at the cost of his own bid. The diamond suit was certainly safe and solid, and the top two honors were cashed. West played his two middle spots, and North was thrilled to unload his ten and six. Now came the diamond nine, as West took the Queen, and North ditched the four, while East discarded the heart ten. The heart nine was now lead; North ducked with the five, and East flew with the Ace. (South played the seven.) North considered taking the chance with one of his heart honors, but chose to play it safe. East then shifted to the Jack of clubs, and South played low as West finessed the Queen. It won, and the attack on hearts continued with the six. This time, North split his honors, and his Jack was followed by the ten, the three, and South's King. Now came the last diamond by South, and North shed his high heart as East shed a club.

Having taken three tricks, South now tossed out his club King, which was won by West as North played his middle spot. West was reduced to all trumps, and played his four. North covered with the eight, as East played low. South took the nine and played the King of trump. The nil was in the clear as North would be able to unload his ten no matter what West did. As thus, the nil rolled home as everyone made their bids. South's Kings, which were limited at the beginning of the hand, rose to the occasion!

DEFENSIVE PLAY AND TECHNIQUES

Defense is one of the essential elements of the game of Spades. While it is imperative to fulfill your contracts, it is equally compelling to defend the opponents' bids properly. Many a game is lost by poor or improper technique which allows impossible nils or borderline contracts to be successfully made. Your Primary Directive (as they say on "Star Trek — The Next Generation") is to make your bid with minimal bagging. However, if you are in danger of defeat (set) or you have already been set, you must switch your attention to defense. The time has come to attack your opponents' contract. Of course, the best of everything is the completion of your bid and defeat of the opponents' bid at the same time, which happens occasionally and produces a wonderful feeling of accomplishment.

As mentioned previously, the greatest opportunity to set the opponents is when the **total of all tricks bid equals 12 or 13.** This allows for the minimal accumulation of bags. After you ensure your contract, you can go for the set with complete confidence. If the total number of tricks exceeds 13 (which happens occasionally with aggressive bidding), it provides "every man for himself" scenario. In this case, once you make your bid, the opponents now are set. To be an outstanding defender, you must also be an aggressive player. The old adage, "the best defense is a good offense" certainly does apply. In Spades, there is no dummy hand, and no specific suit or no-trump bids. Thus, you must interpret information by analyzing the opponents' plays, signals, and discards. **Your partner is the most important part of your defensive effort.** If you just sit there, and ignore the meanings of his plays and discards, you greatly diminish your chance of a successful defense. The road to a successful defense begins with the **opening lead.**

The game of Spades is relatively new when compared to Bridge. Plenty of books have been written about Bidding Systems, and Play of the Hand. While some of these do have a true relevance to Spades, most are merely useful guidelines. Defense is a different proposition, and its strategy is universal.

OPENING LEADS

When the round of bidding is over, the player on the left hand side of the dealer makes the opening lead. He must think in a dual fashion — how can I ensure my team's contract, and how can I set the opponents' contract? The best players in the world do not always make the best lead — but they are savvy enough to be familiar with the combinations and percentages which produce results. Opening leads are not exercises in clairvoyance or serendipity. There are logical and straightforward techniques. Lastly, we must consider leads against nil bids, as well as leads against numerical (non-nil) contracts. Incidentally, if you are on lead against **your partner's nil bid,** this is part of "covering" or protecting his nil. We discussed this in an earlier section.

Here are some useful and general "tips" for leads against "standard" or numerical contracts. If you have a **singleton** in a side suit, lead it. The only exception to this is the lead of a singleton King which may give a free trick to the offense.*

A. Lead the top card from any doubleton such as the nine, three or Ace six. This applies to spot card doubletons or Ace doubletons only. When you lead with a spot card and then play a lower spot card of the same suit in the next round, your partner is alerted that you are now void in that suit. In Bridge, this is called a "high– low" or "echo" signal.

B. Lead the King from any sequence combination including King-Queen or Ace-King. Refer to opening lead table at end of this chapter.

C. Do not underlead Aces, Kings, or Queens.

D. It is acceptable to lead a weak neutral suit consisting of spot cards if you do not have a comfortable alternative; e.g., if you hold 9 8 7 of a suit, lead the 7. If you then play the 8 on the next round, partner now knows that you started with at least three cards in that suit.

DEFENSE AGAINST NIL BIDS

Defending the enemy's nil bid can be a very daunting task. Some players are absolutely intimidated when they hear the word "nil" from either opponent. If all nils were sound, then we would not waste our time defending them. As I said before, most nils have an "underbelly" — and it can be exposed with proper defense. Remember, you are working with a partner and good communication is vital.

A nil is a trick-avoidance bid; therefore, the defense should also think in reverse. The partner of the nil bidder will be doing everything he can to ensure the success of the nil — and this includes sacrificing his own bid, if necessary. A lot of "botched" nils are due to poor cooperation between the nil bidder and his partner. Your job is to confuse the nil bidder or his partner and induce an erroneous play. Here are some useful tips for "breaking" the opponents' nils: Remember, it is important to make your high level bids (seven or more), and the score will dictate your

---

* "Bag" count and score will often dictate opening leads.

options. Low bids at the one to four level can and should be sacrificed if the nil can be attacked efficiently.

"NIL-BUSTING" (TEN "EASY" STEPS)

1. If you have the opening lead, and you hold a long **sequence of low cards** in the **same** suit, begin your attack here. This will force the nil bidder's partner to use his "covering" cards in the same suit prematurely. An alternative is the lead of middle cards, but this is much less effective.

2. A very strong defense is the lead of a **singleton or doubleton** — especially if it is a spot card. This will prepare for the **breaking of trump** — a very vital part of the defense. In addition, you (the defender) will now be able to discard other useless high (or middle) cards. You might even get "lucky" and catch a stranded high card in the nil bidder's hand.

3. Do not lead or cash high cards in suits which are **lengthy**. This will allow the nil bidder to discard losers, and will accumulate bags for you, as well.

4. If your partner leads with a low card, and the nil bidder's partner also plays low (for any reason), then it is vital to play your lowest card as well. The nil bidder may be forced to win this trick.

5. If you hold one or two (**and no more**) middle high cards in a suit, and do not have a natural low-card lead, by all means, get these "puppies" out of the way. Please note that this must be done very **early** in the hand before either opponent has a chance to discard in this suit. Although some "strategists" will argue against this technique, I am prepared to defend this maneuver. I cannot see the value of leaving a high singleton or doubleton combination of cards in your hand, while shifting to another suit.

6. The most effective defense against a nil is the **"breaking"** and **controlled subsequent lead of spades**. The idea is to **remove the trump from the partner of the nil bidder**, and prevent possible ruffs in weak suits. This can be a very delicate maneuver, as you do not want to allow a critical discard on excessive spade leads. Leads of middle and

then low spades are quite good, and may flush out an exposed spade honor or weak middle card, such as the nine or ten from the nil bidder's hand. There is always a risk in "flushing trump" however, experience has shown that it is a good strategy against nils.

7. Do not lead a suit in which the nil bidder is void. This is a horrible play, and allows for easy discards.

8. Another equally putrid play is the yielding of a "**ruff-sluff**". This occurs after the lead of any suit in which both of the opponents are void, and usually occurs toward the middle or end of the hand. (The nil bidder makes a discard while his partner trumps or the nil bidder underruffs his partner's higher trump.)

9. If your side has a contract of **eight or more tricks** on the table, **your strategy should shift.** The first priority is the success of your bid. If the nil appears to be impregnable, his "partner" may be vulnerable. He will be conceding tricks early in the hand, which may weaken his own bid. Most importantly, he cannot expect any support from a nil-bidding partner — who is in no position to offer any help! Should his bid be in the range of three-five tricks (with an eight or nine trick contract by your side), by all means, go for the **set of the nil bidder's partner.** As we said previously, when the combined total of tricks equals 12 or 13 — it is worthwhile going for the set. This is one of the very few instances in which an enemy nil bid is ignored. Another example occurs when the nil bid is inconsequential, and your side will win the game or amass a huge lead — even if the nil makes.

10. A very sound technique is the use of the "high-cut". Ruffing with high trump early in the hand may promote a middle trump in the Nil hand. (The partner may not be able to cover the winning spade.) However, you must consider your contract and the score at the time before utilizing this strategy.

STANDARD OPENING LEAD SUMMARY
(AGAINST STANDARD-NUMERICAL BID-CONTRACTS)

CARDS HELD	SUGGESTED LEAD
A K Q (x)	King
A K Q J	King
A K J(x)	King
A K xxx	King
A Q x(x)	Do not lead from this holding
K Q J	King
K Q x(x)	King
Kxx(x)	Do not lead from this holding
Q J 10(x)	Queen
Q Jx(x)	Do not lead from this holding
J 10 9x	Jack

Please note that these leads do not apply against nil bids. If your partner has bid nil, the lead of a very long and strong suit is ideal. If either opponent has bid nil, your best lead is a middle or low card. (Refer to review of "nil" defense).

The following chart is a classic example of what appears to be a sound nil bid; however, the spade length is a bit suspect. North/South were losing by 150 points and their situation was desperate. We still would recommend this nil bid anyway as partner probably could help with one spade honor and the other spades could be used for underruffing. The opening lead was the Queen of clubs, followed by the nine, King and seven. Now the eight of diamonds was pushed. North played the seven, East covered with the King, and South ducked, saving the Ace for nil protection. East trotted out the ten of diamonds and South inserted the Ace as West trumped with the Jack and north dumped his Queen of diamonds. A small spade was played by West to his partner's Queen and another diamond was returned. South covered with the Jack and West trumped with the Ace of spades. The King of spades was cashed, as East played the nine. The Queen of hearts was led, North played the ten, East played the eight and South played low. The nine of hearts was played, North dropped the three, East played the seven and South took the Jack. Everything looked fine except for one small detail. North had two trumps remaining, East had one and the nil was doomed. This is just one of those unfortunate situations which does occur and is comparable to a "fix" in bridge. Basically, your play is correct, yet the results are unfavorable due to the distribution of the cards and power of the trump suit. We will observe an extreme example of this theme later on in this book.

ILLUSTRATIVE HAND #15 — "MAMA SAID THERE'LL BE DAYS LIKE THIS"

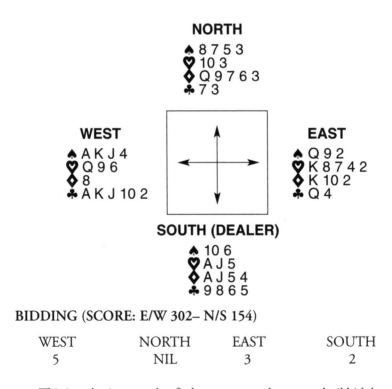

NORTH
♠ 8 7 5 3
♥ 10 3
♦ Q 9 7 6 3
♣ 7 3

WEST
♠ A K J 4
♥ Q 9 6
♦ 8
♣ A K J 10 2

EAST
♠ Q 9 2
♥ K 8 7 4 2
♦ K 10 2
♣ Q 4

SOUTH (DEALER)
♠ 10 6
♥ A J 5
♦ A J 5 4
♣ 9 8 6 5

BIDDING (SCORE: E/W 302– N/S 154)

WEST	NORTH	EAST	SOUTH
5	NIL	3	2

This is a classic example of what appears to be a sound nil bid; however, the spade length is a bit suspect. North/South were losing by 150 points and their situation was desperate. We still would recommend this nil bid anyway as partner probably could help with one spade honor and the other spades could be used for underruffing. The opening lead was the King of clubs, followed by the nine, Queen and seven. Now the eight of diamonds was pushed. North played the seven, East covered with the King, and South ducked, saving the Ace for nil protection. East trotted out the ten of diamonds and South inserted the Ace as West trumped with the Jack and North dumped his Queen of diamonds, A small spade was played by West to his partner's Queen and another diamond was returned. South covered with the Jack and West trumped with the Ace of spades. The King of spades was cashed, as East played the nine. The Queen of hearts was led, North played the ten, East played the eight and South played low. The nine of hearts was played, North dropped the three, East played the seven and South took the Jack. Everything looked fine except for one small detail. North had two trumps remaining, East had one and the nil was doomed. This is just one of those unfortunate situations which does occur and is comparable to a "fix" in bridge. Basically, your play is correct, yet the results are unfavorable due to the distribution of the cards and the power of the trump suit. We will observe an extreme example of this theme later on in this book.

ILLUSTRATIVE HAND #16 — "JACK ATTACK"

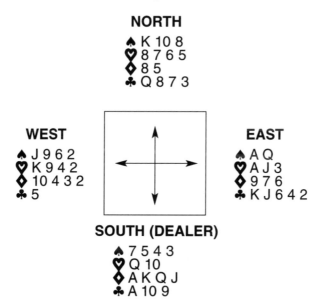

NORTH
♠ K 10 8
♥ 8 7 6 5
♦ 8 5
♣ Q 8 7 3

WEST
♠ J 9 6 2
♥ K 9 4 2
♦ 10 4 3 2
♣ 5

EAST
♠ A Q
♥ A J 3
♦ 9 7 6
♣ K J 6 4 2

SOUTH (DEALER)
♠ 7 5 4 3
♥ Q 10
♦ A K Q J
♣ A 10 9

BIDDING (SCORE: E/W 403– N/S 354)

WEST	NORTH	EAST	SOUTH
3	3	4	4

The bidding was routine, and South, with the last call , felt compelled to bid four (to avoid a ten point loss).However, this created this somewhat peculiar situation of both sides bidding seven! The total of 14 tricks condemned someone to failure and so it became a ferocious battle. Incidentally, this is the type of hand that you would see in the variation of spades referred to as "homicide." The total number of tricks in the homicide variation must equal 14 and the final bidder is required to ensure that total. We need to review two of the bids. West was somewhat aggressive as he hoped to score his King of hearts and two trump. North was very aggressive as he hoped to score his Queen of clubs and two trump. East's bid is very reasonable and South had a good shot at fulfilling his as well, especially with the extra spade and three top tricks. West opened an obvious five of clubs, North played low and East's Jack (a wonderfully imaginative finesse) was taken by the Ace. South now started the diamond suit and was pleased to take three rounds as his partner discarded a heart on the third round. Having fulfilled his bid, South now continued with a fourth round of diamonds and his partner could not resist trumping with the eight (a very odd play), as East took his Queen of spades. The Ace of spades was cashed with everyone following, as West was quite pleased to see the ten drop. East paused to take the King of clubs as West played a low heart. Now the Ace of hearts was dropped on the table, followed by a small heart to the King. A low spade was returned to North's King. The critical junction was reached. Each side had five tricks. North now tried a heart. East's Jack was trumped by South, and the last two tricks were scored by the Jack and nine of trump. The final result was East/West seven tricks; North/South six tricks (and defeat). We really have to appreciate the absolutely brilliant play of the Jack of clubs on the first trick. How could East have known the importance of this play? This was truly a memorable hand.

THE ENDGAME IN SPADES

The term "Endgame" is borrowed from the game of Chess. It indicates the stage of play in which most of the pieces have been exchanged, and the board is relatively clear. A typical example would be a King, a Rook, and three Pawns against a King, a Rook, and two Pawns. Now positional play becomes vital, as each side tries to occupy crucial squares and calculate offensive or defensive maneuvers.

In Spades, the "Endgame" begins when both sides have reached the 400 point plateau, and/or the goal of 500 points is now in sight. Sometimes nil bids will become a factor before the 400 point level is reached. Double nils (cheap shot bids) are desperation efforts (reminiscent of The Battle of The Bulge/Bastogne, 1944!), and are not worthy of discussion here! Here are some very important endgame considerations:

A. Your score

B. Their score

C. Bag count for each side

D. The number of points needed by each team to win the game

E. The optimum contract needed to ensure a win.

Let us look at some examples:

A. The opponents are ahead 445 to 441. You are the dealer (South) and you pick up this hand:

♠ A 5 ♥ A Q 7 5 2 ♦ 6 5 3 ♣ A 8 7

The bidding has proceeded as follows: West — three; North (your partner) —three; and East — three. You have three solid tricks in your hand, with the possibility of winning a heart finesse with the Queen for a fourth trick. Of course, if your partner comes up with the heart King, or the finesse loses, you will probably be limited to your heart Ace. (A bad lie of the suit may result in your taking no heart trick at all!)

Now you must decide what to do. You cannot "bag out" the ops unless you go set — a rather remote possibility. A safe bid of three is plausible. However, this forces you to set the opponents; otherwise, if both teams make their bids, you will lose 505 to 501 (the bag does not matter here). A much better choice for you is the **bid of four**! Now the successful combined bid of seven by your team scores 511 points — regardless of what the opponents do. If you go set, they will have won anyway. Some players call this "Power Bidding"; others have used the term "Bidding to Win."

Now, let us go back to the above example. This time, the opponents are leading with a score of 449 to 434. You have been dealt the same hand. The bidding is identical, with three consecutive three bids coming to you in fourth seat. What is your strategy now?

The opponents' nine bag count is a very inviting target. You really have only two possible choices: a. bid five (and hope to make a team combined bid of eight for a score of 514 and a set of the opponents — a rather tall order) or b. bid three (or even two) for a combined bid of six or five — with the idea of "bagging" out the ops and positioning your side with a score in the 480s or 490s. This drops the opponents to the low 400s and virtually forces them to bid nil on the next hand.

Note that a bid of **four** by you is very poor, as you both may score your team contracts, and your side is a loser by a score of 509 to 504! Another gruesome alternative is going set while bagging out the opponents!

Thus (b.) is the best choice.

B.   Here is another interesting example:

You are breezing along with a lead of 464 to 412. You are sitting South, with this holding:

♠ K Q 8 6   ♥ A 10 9 8 5   ♦ VOID   ♣ K Q 10 9

West is the dealer, and your partner opens with a four, and the East player jolts you with a nil! Your hand is a good bet for four tricks, especially with the void suit. A three bid is much too conservative, and gives West too much room! This is not a bagging situation, and furthermore, your hand is not very favorable for attacking the nil. Now you decide to do some quick math! 464 + 40 + 40 = 544. The West player is also cagey, and knows that he, too, can bid four in this scenario. 412 + 100 (Nil) + 40 = 552. And that is just enough for the city! It is really amazing just how many games are won or lost by a few bags!

Suppose you bid an aggressive, but reasonable, **five**. Now your math computes as follows: 464 + 40 + 50 = 554. The West player, with the last bid, is in a pickle. His planned four bid (making the total 13) loses to a successful combined nine bid by your side. Thus, he is forced to consider a five bid of his own (412 + 100 + 50 = 562). Thus, he will face the daunting prospect of covering his partner's nil, and making his bid. If your partner is a reliable bidder, you have an excellent chance of knocking out the covering bid. (The nil is immaterial here, and you could care less if it makes).

C. Here is the final example:

You are sitting in the good old South seat, and you are the dealer. The opponents are winning 435 to 402. You hold:

♠ K 2   ♥ Q 9 5 2   ♦ K J 9 3 2   ♣ 6 3

West opens with a bid of three, and your partner bids four. East also bids four, and you realize that the opponents are threatening to win the game. What is your call?

You **must** bid nil, and hope that your partner holds the spade Ace (a 33 percent probability). Yes, the heart suit is also suspect, and will require a favorable layout. The alternative bid of one is very weak, and tantamount to surrender. Opponents are a lock for their seven bid, and you may not even make a one bid, if the Ace of spades is on the left, or clubs aren't led early.

Endgame analysis is a key to winning Spades games. Always be aware of the score, and the bag count!

ILLUSTRATIVE HAND #17 — "THE MERRIMACK COUP"

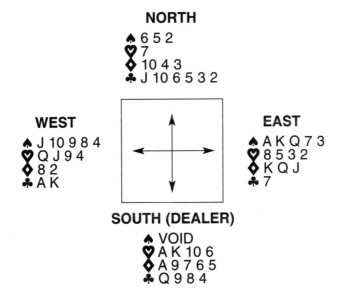

NORTH
♠ 6 5 2
♥ 7
♦ 10 4 3
♣ J 10 6 5 3 2

WEST
♠ J 10 9 8 4
♥ Q J 9 4
♦ 8 2
♣ A K

EAST
♠ A K Q 7 3
♥ 8 5 3 2
♦ K Q J
♣ 7

SOUTH (DEALER)
♠ VOID
♥ A K 10 6
♦ A 9 7 6 5
♣ Q 9 8 4

BIDDING (SCORE: E/W 406– N/S 373)

WEST	NORTH	EAST	SOUTH
5	NIL	5	3

This is a very neat hand featuring a rarely seen maneuver. The United States Civil War featured a very famous sea battle between the first two iron-clad ships — the North had the Monitor, and the South had the Merrimack. Although the engagement ended in a draw, the South later scuttled their ironclad ship — rather than have it fall into Union hands. The ship was also sacrificed in order to blockade a harbor. Plenty of literature is available about the famous battle and its impact on future ship design.

In this hand, the North player decides to intentionally "sink" his bid — as he realizes that a successful nil leads to a loss. This most peculiar play is called the "Merrimack Coup," and is a very strategic play.

The bidding is very logical. West and East have very good play for their five bids, and the North nil is quite safe, with a very minimal risk (the heart seven). South is in a quandary. He has virtually no play for a four bid, and must hope to set the E/W contract, as well as covering his partner's nil — a tall order indeed! If both sides make their respective bids, E/W will win by a score of 506 to 503.

Ignoring the Nil, West cashes the Ace-King of clubs, as North tosses the Jack and ten, and East unloads a low heart and his lone (club) seven spot. South releases the nine and four. West now trots out the diamond four, as North immediately plays his ten spot — hoping for an honor card in his partner's hand. East resolves the matter, as he flies with the King, and South grabs the Ace. The heart suit is logical continuation, and the Ace and King are cashed by South. East and West follow low twice, and North ditches the diamond four on the second heart trick. The heart ten is now continued, as West covers with the Queen.

North now pauses for thought. It is quite obvious that the South hand is spent. He cannot hold the diamond Queen, as he certainly would have tried for a fourth trick (and a set) instead of leading the heart ten. Surely East and West must hold the top trump, and lots of them, too — in order to justify their five bids. As soon as trump are led, East and West will have all top winners, as well as the side cards in red suits. Accordingly, the Queen of hearts is ruffed with the spade deuce, as North "scuttles" his Nil! This move sets the E/W contract as well, and gains 30 points for the N/S Team. The game is thus prolonged, and N/S have a new life! The "Merrimack Coup" provides a second chance!

THE FINESSE

A FINESSE IS AN ATTEMPT TO WIN A TRICK WITH A LESSER CARD. THIS technique has been a standard part of many card games such as Bridge and Whest. Suppose you need two tricks to fulfill your contract or to set the opponents. You are coming down to the end of a hand. You hold the Ace and Queen of hearts. Your partner, who has already made his bid, leads the eight of hearts, your right hand opponent plays the nine in normal cadence (we will come to the topic of hesitations later in this section). What do you do? If you take your Ace, you will lose the Queen to the King no matter which opponent holds the monarch. Your partner probably does not hold the King as he already has made his bid and would not under lead that card. Another indication is his lead of a heart, which is probably a neutral suit. Your best chance (50 percent) is to play the Queen. If the left hand opponent has the King you would have lost it anyway. However, if your right hand opponent has the King, the Queen will win the trick, and you will score your Ace on the next round of hearts. Although 50 percent is not a guarantee, it is far better than 0 percent. Should you hold the same A–Q combination in spades your likelihood of winning two tricks with a successful finesse is guaranteed.

Finesses come in all types and shapes. There is the common (A-Q) specimen, as well as the rare "ruffing" variety (K-Q-J opposite a void).

Suppose you hold K x or K x x of a suit. Partner has already made his bid; you are in need of one more trick to make yours. A lead from your left hand opponent is ideal — as you will get to play the King in fourth position or duck if the Ace shows up. If your partner or right hand opponent leads this suit, and the Ace does not appear, you must play the King. If you play small your left hand opponent may win the trick with the Queen; thus, your best chance is to play the King. Why? Well, if your left hand opponent has the Ace, your King was dead anyway. If your partner has the Ace your King is the winner (it is unlikely that your partner held the Ace in this situation as he has already made his bid). The key is your right hand opponent — and if he holds the Ace, your King wins. If your right hand opponent leads a small card of this suit, an exception to the "second hand low" adage applies. At this point, you must play the King and hope that your left hand opponent does not hold the Ace. There are also situations in a close contract where the play of the King will promote the Queen for your partner if he happens to hold her. If the Ace and Queen are on your left, your King would be dead anyway unless your left hand opponent grabbed the Ace earlier in the hand. We cannot always expect our opponents to do our work for us. There are instances where we will win ("free" finesses) and these usually occur when the left hand opponent underleads his honor cards and allows you to score a King or A–Q combination. There is an impulse to grab your top tricks and sometimes this is correct especially if you are avoiding bags. However, there are many situations where you will need to manufacture a trick, and a finesse is a convenient way to accomplish this. Here is a table of finessing scenarios and the proper card to play. Assume a small card has been led, and it is your turn to play.

*** FINESSING GUIDELINE CHART ***

# of Tricks Needed	You Hold These Cards	Lead From Right Hand Opponent or Partner*	Proper Play (Specific Card)	Comment
2	A Q x	X	Q	Only if you need two tricks or are trying to set the opponents
2	A Q xx (x)	X	Q	Slightly higher risk with longer hold-
2	A Q xxx	X	A	With a long suit, take the Ace and forget the finesse
1	K x	X	K	Your only chance
1	K xx	X	K	Your only chance
1	K xxx (x)	X	K	It's now or never!
2	A Q 10	X	Q	Correct, if only two tricks are needed
3	A Q 10 x	X	10	Your only hope is that K J are on the right — called a "double" finesse
2	K Q x (x)	X	K	Your best chance
1	K J xx (x)	X	K	Similar to above example
2	K J x (x)	X	J	You must hope A Q are on right
3	A K J (x)	X	J	Desperate situation
2	A K J x (x)	X	A	Forget about three tricks!
2	A J 10 (x)	X	J	Standard technique / "repeating" finesse

*Assume that RHO plays a spot card in second seat.

SUMMARY OF FINESSES

Review the finessing guide table above and commit to memory the basic combinations listed. Please note that in some instances you may have to surrender the lead in order to repeat the finesse in the same suit at a later interval. The purpose of the finesse is to try to establish and promote tricks with lesser cards and it may provide salvation in an otherwise lost situation. It is also essential to consider when to finesse and when not to finesse. Long suits reduce the potential for successful finesses. It is particularly aggravating to take a losing finesse, e.g., with an A–Q combination and then have your Ace trumped on the next round leaving you with nothing. The objective is to ensure your contract without becoming finesse-happy. Another very important consideration is the accumulation of bags. Therefore, use the finesse wisely but do not become overly dependent on it. The wreckage of many "overfinessed" hands is littered on the reefs and shoals of the "Island of Spades."

MISCELLANEOUS: RARE FINESSES:

A.   Ruffing Finesses:

Once in a while, we see relatively rare finesses. It is quite possible to finesse an Ace! Look at this layout:

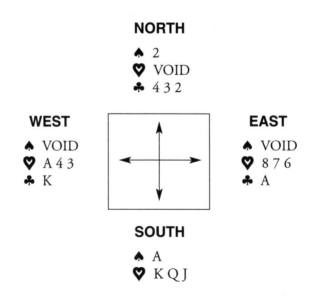

NORTH
♠ 2
♥ VOID
♣ 4 3 2

WEST
♠ VOID
♥ A 4 3
♣ K

EAST
♠ VOID
♥ 8 7 6
♣ A

SOUTH
♠ A
♥ K Q J

North/South are in need of all of the remaining tricks. South (on lead), knows that his partner has the last trump (in addition to his own Ace). He also knows that his partner trumped an earlier heart lead; therefore, the heart Ace is held by one of his opponents. If East holds the Ace, there is nothing South can do. If West holds it, then there is a chance.

Cashing the spade Ace is useless, as the next lead surrenders a heart to **whomever** holds the Ace. However, the lead of the heart King works wonders. If West plays low, then South lets his heart lead "ride." As the cards lie, he is rewarded, as long as his partner does not carelessly ruff. (The lead of the King should be enough of a deterrent.) Now the finesse is repeated, and if West ducks again, North throws another of his minor suit spot cards. Finally, the third lead of hearts smothers the Ace, and the rest are taken quite easily. If West covers the first heart lead with his Ace, then North ruffs with his low trump, and leads any card — which South promptly ruffs. Now his hand is high, and he claims the rest. Ruffing finesses can work with any sequential honor card combination, as long as your partner is void and has the discipline to control the urge to trump. However, you must remember that a finesse is only a 50 percent proposition. And the longer your suit — the greater the risk!

B. Trump Coup — "En Passant"

The rarest finesse is the "En Passant" variety — in Bridge, this may occur once every two hundred hands. In Spades, it is the rarest play. It reminds me of the "Soderlund Squeeze" in the game of Hearts. I have seen five or six "En Passant" plays in the past twenty years. Here is the basic position (typical layout).

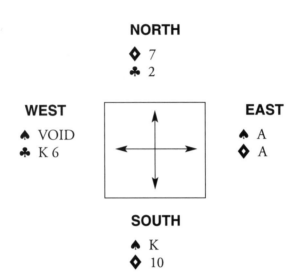

NORTH

♦ 7
♣ 2

WEST

♠ VOID
♣ K 6

EAST

♠ A
♦ A

SOUTH

♠ K
♦ 10

In this basic two-card end position, North is on lead, and he knows that his partner and East are void in clubs. The heart suit has already been exhausted, and his side has lost two diamond tricks to the King and Queen — a very strong indication that the enemy holds the Ace as well (as it has not been played). His side needs one more trick in order to fulfill a game-winning contract. Finally, he knows that the Ace and King of spades are still out. Obviously, if his partner has the trump Ace, then all is well. If his partner holds neither trump honor, then it is lights out! Thus, the King of trump is the key card, and North must make the right lead and allow the possibility that East has the Ace.

A diamond is useless, as West is marked with the remaining two clubs, therefore East has the Ace, and South has the last one. In that scenario, East would grab the Ace of diamonds, and drop South's trump King with the spade Ace. **However, a club lead words wonders!** If East trumps with his master spade, South merely throws off his diamond, and now the King of spades is promoted and ruffs East's diamond on trick #13! If East chooses instead to jettison his diamond Ace on the club lead, then South ruffs immediately, and cheerfully concedes his diamond ten to East's Ace on the last trick. What a pretty line! If the E/W hands are reversed , South would be in deep trouble!

ILLUSTRATIVE HAND #18 — "FINESSER'S DELIGHT"

NORTH (DEALER)

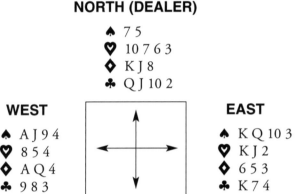

NORTH (DEALER)
- ♠ 7 5
- ♥ 10 7 6 3
- ♦ K J 8
- ♣ Q J 10 2

WEST
- ♠ A J 9 4
- ♥ 8 5 4
- ♦ A Q 4
- ♣ 9 8 3

EAST
- ♠ K Q 10 3
- ♥ K J 2
- ♦ 6 5 3
- ♣ K 7 4

SOUTH
- ♠ 8 6 2
- ♥ A Q 9
- ♦ 10 9 7 2
- ♣ A 6 5

BIDDING (SCORE: TIED AT 300 EACH)

WEST	NORTH	EAST	SOUTH
5	2	3	2

This hand illustrates the wonderful trick taking power of middle cards. In Bridge, great emphasis is placed on the value of middle cards such as J 10 9s. Once in a while a Spades hand occurs in which this theme is emphasized. The bidding was normal, although West's bid was slightly conservative and North was slightly aggressive. The score was tied and bags were immaterial.)The score was 300 points each. East led his safe three of diamonds and South played the ten. West tried the first finesse of the hand with his Queen and North snagged the King. The club Queen was now trotted out and after a long pause, East covered with the King. This was a very dubious play as it allowed South to have access to his partner's hand. The club Ace won the trick and the club layout was quite clear. Now the heart suit was about to be explored. South led a small club and

North won his Jack. The heart 10 was played and once again, East hesitated (and played the deuce) — a dead giveaway. South brilliantly deposited his nine under his partner's ten and was quite pleased with the result. The heart seven was now played and East's Jack was taken by South's Queen as West followed low. The heart Ace cleared the suit as everyone followed and East finally dropped his King. Three suits were now resolved and South proceeded to cash out his remaining winners. Another high club was taken by North. With seven tricks already in the bank, South now went for the set. A low diamond was led and West flew with his Ace. The forced diamond return (spades was still "unbroken") was taken by North's Jack. At this point, North/South cheerfully conceded the remaining five tricks and East/West were defeated. The key to this hand was the trick taking power of the middle cards and the very opportunistic play of North/South. If we reverse the East/West hands the results are entirely different. Now East/West will score one club, at least one heart, two diamonds, and four trump. And North/South must scramble to make their contract!

ILLUSTRATIVE HAND #19 — "WHOOPS"

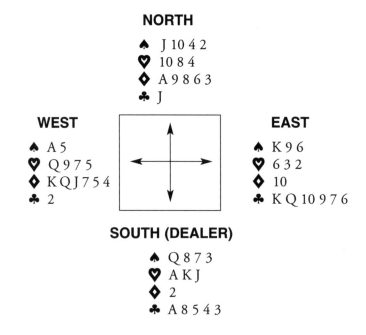

NORTH
♠ J 10 4 2
♥ 10 8 4
♦ A 9 8 6 3
♣ J

WEST
♠ A 5
♥ Q 9 7 5
♦ K Q J 7 5 4
♣ 2

EAST
♠ K 9 6
♥ 6 3 2
♦ 10
♣ K Q 10 9 7 6

SOUTH (DEALER)
♠ Q 8 7 3
♥ A K J
♦ 2
♣ A 8 5 4 3

BIDDING (SCORE: N/S 426 – E/W 444)

WEST	NORTH	EAST	SOUTH
2	3	2	5

This hand was observed in a Worldplay (AOL) event back in 1997. There are some really intricate and intriguing lines of play. See for yourself. . . .

West opened the bidding with a two, and North aggressively bid three. East contemplated a Nil, but the spade King and nine were deterrents, and the club suit was very suspect. As the cards lie, Nil can be made only by very poor defense. South stretched for a five bid, as the opportunity to close out the game with eighty points was just too difficult to resist.

West led the club deuce, followed by the Jack, King and South's Ace. Now South led his singleton diamond, and West played the King, while North covered with the Ace. (East followed with his spot card.) North continued with the diamond three, as East very cleverly discarded a low HEART, and South ruffed with the trump three, as West disgustingly pitched the Jack. The three of clubs was placed on the table which North trumped with the deuce (West tossed a low diamond). Another low diamond followed, and East once again disdained trumping, as he unloaded another heart! South gurgled gleefully as he ruffed with his seven, and West followed with his seven. "Far out" proclaimed South, and he played another low club, as West discarded his lowest heart, and North trumped with the four. The diamond eight drew a small heart discard by East and a ruff with South's eight, while West followed. A low club lead by South allowed West to unload another low heart and North now ruffed with he ten, as East played the ten.

Now the moment of truth had arrived. North/South had already scored seven tricks, and the lead of North's last diamond threatened to let the spade Queen win *"en passant"*. (an extremely beautiful play!) Instead, East rose with the King of spades, and a dumfounded South discarded the heart Jack, as West released his last diamond. The spade six was now played, and the Queen was gobbled up by the Ace as North's Jack also fell! Whoops! The spade five was trotted out, and it went to East's nine — the Master trump. All of the remaining clubs were good, and down went the eight bid. This was a really wild defense, but there is a lot of analysis here.

Do you see where North/South went astray?

The hand clearly called for a cross-ruff, BUT one detail needed attention. This theme often is seen in the game of Bridge, but rarely in Spades. Basically, if you hold a side suit of three cards or less with two winners (e.g. the Ace-King), it is a wise idea to CASH THE SIDE SUIT WINNERS FIRST AND THEN PROCEED WITH THE CROSS-RUFF. East was very careful to discard his heart suit low cards on North's diamond leads — which allowed him the opportunity to ruff hearts if this suit was led. Had South paused to cash the Ace-King of Hearts BEFORE proceeding with the cross-ruff, it would have given him two more vital tricks. Given the fact that he held only three hearts, the odds were favorable of scoring two tricks.

When this hand was first played (in Worldplay), the post-mortems were quite intense! I was kibitzing this hand, and was quite impressed with the analysis presented by the North player. then I spotted the line of defense which could have succeeded.

Had South taken his top hearts and then tried for a club ruff, West had an opportunity to resort to an alternative defense. The second club lead (by South) is ruffed with the Ace! North is now forced to discard a side suit. The spade five would be led, followed by a low spot by North, and the KING by East. The nine of spades would then deprive North/South of two more ruffs. Finally, the minor suit winners into he East/West hands set the contract. The repeated leads of trump have been the antidote for hands which have a distinct cross-ruffing pattern.

How many West players could find such a defense?

Sometimes the most interesting plays are those which are never made in the heat of battle!

TEN SPADES CONVENTIONS AND PARTNERSHIP AGREEMENTS

1. Attitude Leads — You are on lead against the opponents. If you do not have a natural sequential lead, you must make a selection. Leading a low card (deuce through five) of a suit indicates that you have some high card strength in that suit. Leading a middle card (six through nine) indicates that you have a weak suit. NOTE: This cannot be used simultaneously with the "High-Low" count convention.

2. The Big "5" Bid — (The "Carney-DeNino") strategy. If you bid before your partner, a five bid will show that you have either the Ace or King of spades. This will allow your partner to bid a nil safely especially if he has a potential trump loser such as K x, K x x, Q x x, etc. It should be noted that you must have at least 4, 5, or 6 tricks in your hand before you utilize this bid.

3. High-Low Signal — This is a very useful "gadget" that applies to heart, diamond, and club holding. If you hold two and only two cards (from deuce to the Jack) in a particular suit, you play the

higher card first (when the suit is led). On the second round of the same suit, you then play the lower card which indicates to your partner that you can trump the suit in the third round. (e.g., You hold the nine and seven of clubs; your partner plays the Ace; you drop your nine. Your partner plays the King and you drop your seven. Now your partner plays a small club. You have told him that you will be trumping on this round. The signal also works quite nicely if you hold an Ace and a small card in the same suit. This is the ideal doubleton, as it "clears" the suit immediately. NOTE: Do not use this system with K x, as the King is just too valuable a card to discard or lead prematurely.

4. Lead Sequence — (Side suits) The lead of a King promises the Queen in the same suit; the lead of a Queen promises the Jack in the same suit; the lead of an Ace promises a singleton or doubleton in the same suit.

5. Low-High Convention — (Side suits) The lead of low card, followed by a high card in the same suit promises at least three cards in that suit. (Refer to "Attitude Leads")

6. Trump Peter (Echo) — The play of a middle card in trump, followed by a lower spade signals that you have a high trump honor (Ace or King). (Do not confuse with the side suit "high-low" play.)

7. Second Hand Low/Third Hand High — A universal system in which it is proper to play a low card in second position. This forces the third player to use a high card in the same suit. Similarly, "third hand high" requires the player in the third seat to play his highest card in the same suit; otherwise the last (fourth seat player) will win a trick cheaply. In Spades, the exception to this "Rule" is the ducking of tricks to force the opponents to take "bags."

8. Suit Preference Signal — Taken from Bridge, this Convention indicates to partner the specific side suit which contains the likely entry card to your hand. (e.g., If diamonds is the ruffed suit, then a high diamond to the "trumper" requests the lead of a hart (after the ruff). A low diamond requests the return of a club.

9. Trump Lead Flush — After spades have been "broken," the play of a low trump demands that one's partner play the highest trump

possible in third position (unless of course the preceding play was a high spade which could not be covered). The idea is to develop middle spades in the partner's hand or to force out the opponents' spades.

10. Blind Nil Force — This is used only when a pair is more than 150 points in arrears and the opponents have at least 300 point. Premature use of the blind nil bid can result in a hopelessly lost game and will anger the opposition if bid early in the game or in an even position.

Herm Carney of Indianapolis, IN, and Roger DeNino of Springfield, MA, have created some rather ingenious and clever Conventions. I have already listed the "Big 5" bid. Here are some really neat "gadgets"!

CONTRIBUTORS

This page was contributed by Herm Carney of Indianapolis, IN, and Roger DeNino of Springfield, MA.

My partner Herm Carney (Scrubber) and I, Roger DeNino (Mr. Fear not) have been using a few conventions to help communicate information by way of either bids or cards that are played as signals in addition to the standard positive and negative signals. We have found that these few tools help us to win more games (than we lose).

FIVE BIDS

If you bid before your partner, a 5 bid will show that you have either the Ace or King of spades. This will allow your partner to bid more nils safely than he would normally without this information.

Examples of hands that most advance players would not nil with unless it was a desperation bid. Please note that these hands refer only to trump holdings:

King, Queen, or Jack Singleton. It also makes it easy to nil with such hands as K x/K x x/Q x/Q x x and so on.

If you do not have either the Ace or King, you must bid — even if you have a higher natural bid.

An example of a hand for which you must bid 8:

♠ J 10 9 7 4 2; ♥ A; ♦ A K 3; ♣ A K 3.
This hand would normally make at least seven tricks plus.

A good player can avoid many bags if he has to. In addition, a hand like this will often lead to setting the opponents many times.

If a partner bids before you, you bid the hand normally. We have found that this increases the number of nil bids that you can make that you normally would not have bid without this convention.

CARD SIGNAL FOR NILS:

I don't know how many times different partners have trumped a suit that they did not need to whose partner in turn may have gotten set on a low trump because he was out, or another suit partner who could have discarded a low card instead of trumping and have a better coverage in the other suits. We have used a certain sequence of cards to alert partner not to waste his trump.

Whenever the nil bidder plays a lower card (following) — followed by a higher spot, it tells partner he has enough low cards in this suit to duck, and do not waste a trump thinking it will protect him.

Example: You play seven on the first round of the suit followed by an eight or higher tells partner save your trumps, I do not need protection in this suit. It's a signal that you use whenever possible and will increase the amount of nils that you will make.

PSYCHE BIDS

Another neat bid that we sometimes use, is a "Psyche" bid. It has to be used at the right time, and the score of the game makes a big difference along with knowing your opponents. If your opponents' score is 300 you have 200 or less you might want to take advantage of trying it out. The psyche bid can only be used in the third bidding position to avoid misleading a partner.

When the bidding may have gone as follows:

Partner: 3

Opponent: 3

Your bid: With a hand that you may only have a 1, 2, 3 bid, you may try to bid six or seven.

Many opponents will double nil. Even if you get set nine or ten, the opponents most likely will set 200 points plus. I remember when there was a time we used this bid, not only did the opponents get set on Double Nil, but they also received nine bags with the one they already had, amounting to a 300 point loss for them. It turns the game right around.

ILLUSTRATIVE HAND #20 — "SUIT PREFERENCE CONVENTION"

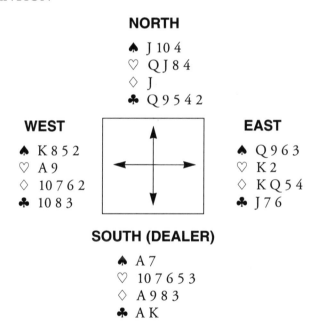

NORTH
- ♠ J 10 4
- ♡ Q J 8 4
- ◇ J
- ♣ Q 9 5 4 2

WEST
- ♠ K 8 5 2
- ♡ A 9
- ◇ 10 7 6 2
- ♣ 10 8 3

EAST
- ♠ Q 9 6 3
- ♡ K 2
- ◇ K Q 5 4
- ♣ J 7 6

SOUTH (DEALER)
- ♠ A 7
- ♡ 10 7 6 5 3
- ◇ A 9 8 3
- ♣ A K

BIDDING (SCORE: N/S 214 – E/W 195)

WEST	NORTH	EAST	SOUTH
3	2	3	4

Another close game was in progress. The bidding was very aggressive, as South made the most reasonable call, and West came off the wall with an outrageous bid! North's two bid left a lot to be desired as well. (Some players with North's hand may have been tempted to bid nil; this could have been tricky with the two trump honors and singleton diamond Jack. West opened with the "powerful" six of diamonds, and North's Jack was covered with the King and South's Ace. After a brief moment of thought, South played the diamond three, eschewing the temptation to cash the club doubleton. West played low, as North trumped with the four, and a surprised East saw his expected diamond trick disappear! Without the slightest hesitation, North returned a club to his partner's King, and another diamond was ruffed — this time with the ten. Finally, a low club from North was taken by South's Ace. A fourth round of diamonds found the spade Jack. Now the coup de grace was administered, as North played another club, and his partner ruffed with the spade seven! South now cashed the trump Ace, and decreed "I'm done," as his partner led his bottom heart. East/West were set, and the price of two bags was well worth it.

It was a rather incredible hand — North/South scored their three top cards in the minor suits, the trump Ace, and four separate ruffs — for a maximum result.

How did North know that a club return was optimal after he ruffed the second round of diamonds? The answer is the Suit Preference Signal, and this is how it words:

In the game of Bridge, the suits have a ranking in this order:

Spades (1st), Hearts (2nd), Diamonds (3rd), and Clubs (last)

Spades is the top suit and Clubs is the lowest suit. In the game of Spades, it is easy to remember this sequence, as Spades are always trump and are the "top dog." Hearts is a major suit, and the minor suits are diamonds and clubs. (If you look at any Bridge column, you see the suits are always ranked in this order.) By the way "No-Trump" does not apply!

Now that we have cleared that out of the way, we will now come to the topic at hand. In the typical trumping or ruffing scenario, there are two factors — the suit which is being trumped, and the trump suit itself. That leaves the other two suits. In order to guide your partner as to **which of the other two suits to return to your hand**, you must help him. There is a perfectly legal way to do so called the Suit Preference Signal. For example, in the illustrated hand, South was leading diamonds for his partner to ruff. South's entry (back to his hand) was the club suit. Therefore, he chose his **lowest diamond** as the indication that his entry was in the **lower ranking side suit. Remember, the trump suit, and the suit which is trumped do not count.** In this case, the two remaining suits were hearts and clubs. If South held the Ace of hearts, he would have returned his highest diamond — the nine — as a signal for his partner to come back to him with a heart.

Here is a quick reference summary: **Spades are always trump, and do not factor into the matrix. If hearts are being ruffed, then the two side suits are diamonds and clubs. A high heart return indicates a possible or sure entry in diamonds; a low heart return indicates a possible or sure entry in clubs. If diamonds are being ruffed, then the two side suits are hearts and clubs. A high diamond return indicates a possible or sure entry in hearts; a low diamond return indicates a possible or sure entry in clubs. Finally, if clubs are being ruffed, then the red suits are the two side suits. A high club indicates a possible entry or sure entry in hearts; a low club indicates a possible or sure entry in diamonds.**

Sometimes the entry will be delayed (instead of the Ace, it may be the King). There are other times where this is no entry at all (no system is perfect). Then you will have those instances where your cards in one of the side suits are winners anyway. In the latter case, you simply cash these out, and allow your partner to discard from another suit. This may set up a ruffing situation in the secondary suit. This is till a nice convention and will pay off quite handsomely in situations where you need tricks for a set or fulfillment of a contract. After all, why have a guess, when you can have a reasonably sure thing? Remember — the more information you can give to your partner — the better your results will be.

ILLUSTRATIVE HAND #21 — "SERENDIPITY"

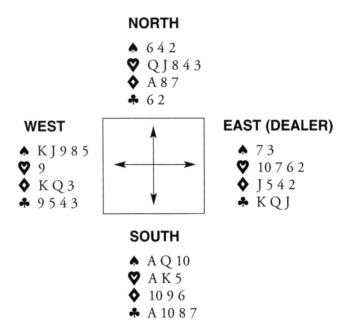

NORTH
♠ 6 4 2
♥ Q J 8 4 3
♦ A 8 7
♣ 6 2

WEST
♠ K J 9 8 5
♥ 9
♦ K Q 3
♣ 9 5 4 3

EAST (DEALER)
♠ 7 3
♥ 10 7 6 2
♦ J 5 4 2
♣ K Q J

SOUTH
♠ A Q 10
♥ A K 5
♦ 10 9 6
♣ A 10 8 7

BIDDING (SCORE: 0–0)

SOUTH	WEST	NORTH	EAST
5	5	1	2

A brief comment on the bidding is in order. It was the first hand of the new game. South's bid of five was quite reasonable, although some players may have chanced a six bid. West's five bid was a bit aggressive, however his trump length was clearly an asset. North's one bid is quite logical and East's bid of two is sound assuming he will take two club tricks. Thirteen tricks were thus bid and the hand became a ferocious tug-of-war between both partnerships. South immediately cashed the Ace of clubs, drawing small spots from West and North, as well as East's King. Now he led his Ace of hearts and followed with the King. The five of spades was played by West and South was jolted. Now he had to manu-facture a trick. West exited with a low club and East took his Queen. Now a third club was pushed and South breathed a sigh of relief as North trumped with a low spade. The heart Queen was led and West ruffed with his spade eight and exited with his King of diamonds. North took his Ace and then played his low diamond as East ducked. West won the Queen and the diamond three went to East's jack. The following position had been reached:

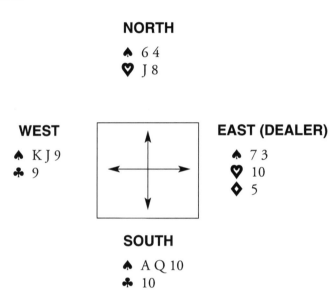

NORTH

♠ 6 4
♥ J 8

WEST

♠ K J 9
♣ 9

EAST (DEALER)

♠ 7 3
♥ 10
♦ 5

SOUTH

♠ A Q 10
♣ 10

East led his heart ten and South pondered the possibility. He chose to discard the club ten instead of trumping. Had South ruffed with the spade ten, West would have overruffed with the Jack and escaped cleanly with his last club. This would have resulted in East trumping with the seven followed by a deadly spade return through South. Instead West now ruffed the heart with his spade nine (otherwise North would have won this trick) and now South was sure to score two tricks. The really pretty play never happened. Suppose West had chosen to discard his club nine after South had discarded his club. North would be on lead with the heart Queen and would have selected a low spade lead. East's play is now immaterial and South would ruff with the ten forcing West to lead into his Ace Queen. This is another delightful example of the end play.

ILLUSTRATIVE HAND #22 — "MAGIC"

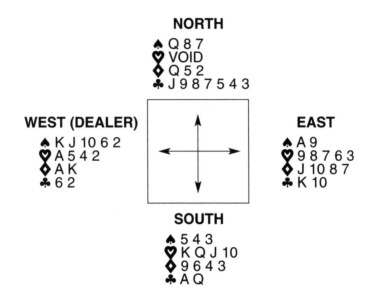

NORTH
♠ Q 8 7
♥ VOID
♦ Q 5 2
♣ J 9 8 7 5 4 3

WEST (DEALER)
♠ K J 10 6 2
♥ A 5 4 2
♦ A K
♣ 6 2

EAST
♠ A 9
♥ 9 8 7 6 3
♦ J 10 8 7
♣ K 10

SOUTH
♠ 5 4 3
♥ K Q J 10
♦ 9 6 4 3
♣ A Q

BIDDING (SCORE: E/W 442 – N/S 392)

SOUTH	WEST	NORTH	EAST
3	5	1	1

East/West were in range of winning, and the only hope appeared to be a "set" — a longshot at best! The bidding was normal, as North feared a trump loser (otherwise a nil was a consideration). East tossed in a conservative one, South counted three winners and trotted out an ambitious three bid. West grabbed at the five bid — he saw at least two trump tricks as well as three red suit winners — and the score of 60 seemed to go along nicely with the 442 already on the board. Anyone looking at the West hand would agree that five tricks were a lead-pipe cinch! West knew his partner could be counted on for one trick. All of the campers were happy. Now it was time for magic!

South (on lead) led the top of his heart sequence. It was a perfectly normal choice; but the Card Gods were about to take over! West hesitated, and finally flew with his Ace. The low spade ruff by North sent a jolt through West! The best was yet to come! North shifted to a low club, and East hesitated before dropping his ten. South read the "hitch" as a club problem (East probably had the King), and his insight proved to be quite correct as he played the club Queen, and the finesse worked. Now the Queen-Jack-ten of hearts were cashed, as East and West helplessly followed suit and North unloaded his three diamonds. South led the diamond three, and poor West watched his Ace get ruffed away! Another club to South's Ace was followed by a diamond lead and another ruff by North. The big "wood" had been felled from the West hand!

By this time, North/South had taken the first EIGHT tricks and the opponents' contract of six was in the tank! The remainder of the hand was cheerfully conceded, and the East/West score dropped by sixty points. The game ended after the next deal.

Was it "Magic"? Was it "Serendipity"? How about "Intuition"? I leave that up to you. All I know is that I had another hand for the book! You just don't see "ruffing finesses" everyday! A rare bird — indeed!

UNCLE JOE'S HOT TIPS

I   BIDDING

1. Your bid is influenced by your opponent's bid, partner's bid and the score of the game. Gauge the strength of your hand accordingly.

2. It is better to bid slightly conservatively rather than risk defeat by overly aggressive bidding.

3. The longer a suit is, the less number of tricks you can expect to take. Do not overvalue lengthy suits or suits with separated honor cards.

4. Do not bid nil if you have more than one prospective loser or separate high trump. An unusually high bid by your partner or the opponents may give you some flexibility.

II   PLAY OF THE HAND

5. Rarely take a trick from your partner unless you have a good reason for doing so.

6. If your partner has bid nil, it is absolutely essential to save your high cards or high spades for the latter stages of the hand (you may have to protect him at a critical time).

7. "Second hand low" is generally good advice, as it gives partner a chance to win a trick. "Third hand high" is also proper as it prevents the last player from winning a trick cheaply. Note: The exception to third hand high is forcing the opponents to take bags.

8. Lead trump as often as possible if you want to set up a solid side suit (called "flushing").

III   DEFENSE

9. The best defense against an opponent's nil bid is the repeated lead of low cards in the side suits — hoping to flush out an Ace or King. Another good strategy is to drain trump from the partner of the nil bidder by leading middle or low spades.

10. Watch your partner's discards and look for encouraging high card signals or discouraging low card signals.

11. Never lead a suit in which both opponents are void. This is called a "ruff-sluff."

12. A safe lead is the top of a sequence (K Q J). A poor play is the underlead of an unprotected honor card or the underlead of an Ace. This may give away a "free finesse."

13. Watch those bags! Once again do not take excess bags in order to set low level bids of less than four.

ETHICS AND COURTESY

It is very important to remember that Spades is only a game and should have no bearing on the real world. You should be polite and courteous with both your partner and your opponents. If your partner succeeds in his bid, a few words of encouragement will go a long way. If your partner makes an error, be understanding and sympathetic. After all, you might make a mistake during the next hand. No one likes to be criticized, berated, or insulted. Repeated displays of sarcasm, bragging, and abusive behavior will result in your playing against computers or by

yourself. At times it may be frustrating to lose, but in Spades, as in life
— that is the way it goes. Finally, it is a very good idea to find a partner with whom you can play on a regular basis. This will help you to
improve your game and develop a rapport. It is a lot more fun to be
competitive and gracious. Remember we all start out as beginners.

BICYCLE
16

DUPLICATE SPADES
STRATEGY AND TECHNIQUE

DUPLICATE IS A FORMAT WHICH HAS BEEN SUCCESSFULLY USED BY THE American Contract Bridge League (ACBL) for several years. The purpose of duplicate is to eliminate the luck of the deal and to **compare your skill to other players holding the same cards.** In this way, the strength of each **partnership can be accurately determined. There are two movements —** **Individuals and Partners.** We will be discussing the Partnership variation.

Each hand is a **separate entity,** and unlike a standard game of 10 deals or 500 points, Duplicate is structured on a complete Round or Match of a **pre-determined number of deals,** or hands. A typical Tournament usually features 28 or 32 deals. You will be assigned a pair number and Direction (North/South or East/West). Then you proceed to your First Round Table. A round will consist of three or four hands. At the end of the round, East/West moves to the next highest numbered Table while North/South remains stationery. Now the play begins!

This is accomplished by the use of a **duplicate board** which, in effect, is a plastic holder for cards. Each board contains **one complete deal.** The deal is separated into four hands, one for each player. Partners still play as a team and sit opposite from each other. The number, direction, and opening bidder are clearly identified. In Duplicate Spades, the **left hand opponent** of the dealer has the **opening bid** and the **first lead** is made by the player to the dealer's immediate **right**. Each board holds a hand record sheet, which allows the verification of a hand to be accomplished easily. There is also a **traveling score** which identifies every contract, final score, and number of tricks and bags taken. Although the bidding is still accomplished in one round, the play of the hand is different. Normally, the cards in a typical "fresh deal game" are thrown into the middle of the table, and the winner of each trick gathers up the four cards (book) and places them in front of himself. In Duplicate, the big difference in the routine is the play of the hand. Instead of tossing the cards into the middle of the table, you simply **turn up each card in front of you.** If your side wins a trick, your card is then turned over vertically. If your side loses a trick your card is turned horizontally. This facilitates the tracking of all tricks when the hand is over and makes it easy to determine the number of tricks taken by each side. A nil bidder taking a trick can be identified quite quickly. The North player is the scorer. The **final score for both partnerships** is recorded on the traveling score sheet and the hand record sheet is quickly checked to determine that the right cards are returned to each pocket. It is always a good idea to double check the scores before the score sheet is returned to the Board. Both forms are then folded and carefully placed in the North pocket of the board (on top of the hand).

Accurate bidding and play is rewarded with a good score. If you underbid, you will be hurt by bags and a lower score. If all pairs bid and make the same score, then the board is a "wash," and everyone receives an average score. If your team has the best score for the board — your side earns a **"top"** — which is terrific! Remember, your performance for each hand is compared to the other pairs in the **same direction** who also played the **same hands!** Nils are always a premium and at the end of the session the scores are then tallied board by board. The method of comparison is called **"match pointing."**

Each hand is a separate entity. Thus, a poor result on one hand can be easily offset by a good result on another. **There are two winners (pairs) for each session.** North/South and East/West produce a representative winner for their Direction(s). This adjusted playoff then pits the two winning partnerships against each other in one final fresh deal game. The **Director** is the person responsible for the event, and if necessary, for mak-

ing any rulings. He is there to help and guide. You will like Duplicate —
as it will allow you to see exactly how well you do against other players.
While the luck of the deal is eliminated, you still have to make the most
of the cards you are holding. It is the measuring standard for Bridge, and
now Spades can move into a new "era" as well! Someday, Duplicate Spades
Clubs will be accessible on a local basis. As of this writing, Duplicate is
available only at National Tournaments. Official updates are available by
referring to: www.classictourneys.com.

BICYCLE

17

LAWS OF SPADES

UNTIL NOW, THE GAME OF SPADES HAS HAD NO PROPER SET OF RULES. WE do realize that there are a plethora of variations and interpretation of rules.

THE PACK

The game of Spades is played with a standard deck of 52 cards and back design, and consisting of 13 cards in each of four suits. The cards in each suit rank downward from the Ace (highest) to the deuce (lowest). The spade suit is designated as trump (outstanding or highest for each hand).

1. NUMBER OF PLAYERS

Three or four may play. There is a two player version referred to as "honeymoon" and the three player version called "individuals or singles." The best game, standard for parties and tournaments is four handed featuring partners. Each partnership consists of two players seated opposite each other. Partners may be determined by previous arrangement or by drawing cards.

THE SHUFFLE, CUT, AND DEAL

These are standard procedural aspects and have been reviewed previously.

2. OBJECT OF THE GAME

The object of the game is to win tricks in quantity to fulfill bid contracts. Points are credited for making contracts and nil bids. A small premium (usually one point each) is also awarded for overtricks. Points are deducted for unsuccessful (set) contracts as well as accumulation of increments of ten overtricks (referred to as "bags"). The game limit for the standard partnership variation is 500 points; the game limit for individuals is 300 points. There is also a negative limit of minus 300 points.

3. OPENING BID/OPENING LEAD

The opening bid is made by the player sitting to the immediate left of the dealer. The opening lead is made by the player seated to the right of the dealer. There are variations for the opening lead. The holder of the deuce of clubs makes the first lead, and the winner of this (first) trick now leads the first card of the second trick. Another variant is having the opening lead initiated by the partner of the dealer. The deal rotates for every hand. There is only one round of bidding and bids are identified by the word nil indicating zero tricks. Blind nil, also indicates zero tricks, and must be made without seeing your hand. There is an option to pass cards (between partners) after a blind nil bid. This must be agreeable to all players at the table. All other bids are stated with a number from 1–13. Suits and no trump are not mentioned. Whoever makes the opening lead must place a card face up on the table; spades may not be led until the trump suit has been discarded or the player on lead has nothing but spades.

4. THE PLAY

After the opening lead, each player in clockwise turn, plays a card and the four cards as played constitute a trick. A player must follow suit if possible. This takes precedence over any other requirement. The player who wins a trick, leads the next trick. If unable to follow suit, a player may play any card which is called a "discard." He also has the option to play a spade which is called "trumping." Any card that is played by placing it face up on the table is determined as "boarded." If such a card is visible to any player or is played in a manner which clearly indicates an intention to play this card, that constitutes a completed action. ("A card seen is a card played.")

5. THE REVOKE (RENEGE)

If a player discards when able to follow suit, he is said to renounce. There is no penalty if he corrects his renounce before any card is played to the next trick. However, if the trick involving the renounce is completed and a card has been played to the next trick, the renounce now becomes a revoke. The penalty for an established revoke is two tricks against the offender; however, the director must be called in order to establish culpability and make a final ruling. If it is determined that a revoke was intentional to avoid taking unwanted tricks, the director may assess a penalty of five bags. (At major events, the penalty for a revoke is loss of bid to the offender)

6. IRREGULARITIES

Any player may call attention to an irregularity. The director should be called at once. If the offender attempts to correct is irregularity he may be further penalized. If two players play a card simultaneously to a trick, the second player is deemed to be in his proper turn. The winner of each trick collects the four cards into a neat packet and lays it face down in front of himself. After the last trick has been played and collected the North player may ask each player who won for verification. If there are any other questions, the director needs to be called.

7. TABLETALKING, MANNERISMS, GESTURES, AND ALL OTHER FORMS OF INAPPROPRIATE BEHAVIOR ARE UNACCEPTABLE. EACH PLAYER IS ASKED TO PLAY COURTEOUSLY ETHICALLY.

8. CLAIMS AND CONCESSIONS

If a player exposes his hand and claims all remaining tricks he must announce the order of his plays. If he fails to announce this any other player may direct how he played his cards. In any case, the director needs to be consulted to make a final ruling. If a player exposes only one card prematurely, this card is deemed to be a lead out of turn and that card must remain on the table and played at next legal opportunity.*

*A/B Productions and ClassicTourneys, Inc. reserve the right to further amend and update these laws.

18

SPADES AND THE INTERNET

THE INCREASED POPULARITY HAS CERTAINLY EXPANDED THE HORIZONS OF card players everywhere. Now any player with a basic computer (and modem) can play a good game of Spades with opponents of all levels. Listed below are three of the best Internet Sites for the game of Spades. (All are free, although there are some other sites which do charge fees.)

A. YAHOO! (WWW.YAHOO.COM)

Yahoo was one of the original "on-line" card game sites, and has been updated. After a brief registration, you will be directed to a general games page, and a click on the Spades link will do the trick! Players of all levels peruse this site, and there are plenty of hosts to help. On-line Tournaments abound — and a series of National "Live" events has been launched by two prominent Yahoo players.

B. MSN GAMING ZONE (WWW.ZONE.COM)

This is one of the oldest of the Classic Card Sites, and by far and away, the largest. It is very nicely formatted, and there are plenty of

Rooms for all levels of play. A very good Ratings system, allows any player to match skills with comparable-strength opponents. There is also a "Ladder" Room for players to compete in a "King of the Mountain" format! You can find a Tournament at almost any time of the day. Game Tips and other articles are regularly featured. A large staff works very hard and there are few problems. Registration is very quick and easy. The Site pioneered the way for others. Plenty of other card and board games are also available.

C. POGO (WWW.POGO.COM)

Here is another nicely formatted Site with an up-to-date design. This is a first-rate operation, which evolved from the original (Cards) Site — "Web Deck." Registration is fast, and you will be playing in a heartbeat! The Classic Cards Section (Spades, Hearts, and Euchre) is well-represented with different levels of competition. There are lots of rooms for beginners, as well as experts. One very unique feature is the "customizing" option, where individuals can select the Rules for their game of choice from a "menu" of options. This is especially helpful for those who might be familiar with a specific variation of their favorite game. Give Pogo. com a look — you will like what they have to offer!

For more information about the "live" National Tournament Series, please e-mail Heartsmoon@aol.com.

D. USPLAYINGCARD.COM

The web site for The United States Playing Card Company will provide an interesting menu with: listing of new and exciting USPC playing card items; history of playing cards; what's new in playing card category; a card games rule section; chat rooms and FAQ's.

For more information about the web site, contact The United States Playing Card Company, located in Cincinnati, Ohio.

SPADES CD'S

Games CDs have been available for many years now. In the good old days of DOS and large "floppies," these were quite the rage! Modern CDs have come a long way! The opportunity to play against "artificial intelligence" is an alternative to the Internet game. Three of the best CDs featuring the game of Spades are:

1. Spades DeLuxe (Freeverse Software; NYC www.freeverse.com) Freeverse Software marketed Hearts Deluxe a few years ago, and now they have produced the Spades Deluxe Program. It will soon be ready for Windows and PC Systems; as of this writing, it is available only for Macintosh Computers. The range of play is from beginner to upper level Intermediate. A lot of creative programming went into the design of this product. The graphics are very clever, and the cute, thematic characters will impress everyone who uses this CD. Directions are easy to follow. For a good, competitive game with a "twist," I suggest that you check this out!

2. Championship Spades (v.7.1) (Dreamquest Software: Lafayette, CO www. dq.com)
    Here is a product which lives up to all of its rave reviews. It is designed for the advanced player who wants to compete on a very high level. The artificial intelligence is the best I have ever seen, and it is truly reminiscent of playing at a National Tournament. Yours truly had to rely on much experience in order to hold my own with this program. If you are practicing for "heavy-duty" competition, give this CD a try! There are multiple variations as well as help with tutorials. You will love the sounds, layout, and rapid-fire play.

3. "Bicycle" Card Collection (Microsoft)
    Release fall of 2000.
    This is first-rate software designed around the world-renowned "Bicycle" playing card brand. The range of play is from novice to expert level of play. Directions are easy with clever characters to help you along the way. Insightful tutorials are also included.

THE SPADES HALL OF FAME

THESE THREE HANDS WILL CLOSE OUT THIS BOOK. THERE WERE PLAYED AT various events (Internet and "live" Tournaments). They represent the highest level of the game, and truly illustrate the ebb and flow of competition under extreme pressure.

It is really wonderful to watch expert Teams in action, and I am sure you will enjoy the display of skill and determination featured in this section.

ILLUSTRATIVE HAND #23 — "THE GREATEST FINESSE OF ALL TIME"

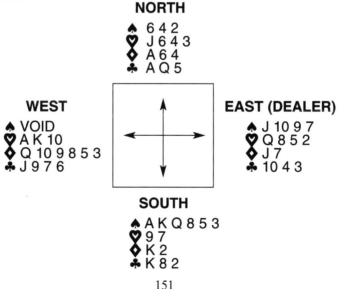

NORTH
♠ 6 4 2
♥ J 6 4 3
♦ A 6 4
♣ A Q 5

WEST
♠ VOID
♥ A K 10
♦ Q 10 9 8 5 3
♣ J 9 7 6

EAST (DEALER)
♠ J 10 9 7
♥ Q 8 5 2
♦ J 7
♣ 10 4 3

SOUTH
♠ A K Q 8 5 3
♥ 9 7
♦ K 2
♣ K 8 2

BIDDING (SCORE: E/W 476 – N/S 412)

SOUTH	WEST	NORTH	EAST
7	2	2	1

This is one of the most exquisite hands ever played. It appeared in a WorldPlay (AOL) Event during the latter part of 1997. I was relatively new to the Premium Games Site, and was waiting for this Round to be completed.

The bidding was quite reasonable, and East had what appeared to be a "Natural" trump trick. South did "stretch" his hand a bit; however, six potential trump tricks and two side Kings, as well as potential ruffing of the red suits certainly justified the call. West cannot be faulted for his two bid as he was reaching for game. North wanted to bid three, but concluded that his "flat" distribution, and two minor suit Aces were worth only two tricks. The club Queen (Finesse) was not a sure thing. Thus, there were twelve tricks on the table. . . .

Now South paused to consider the situation. If East/West completed their contract, the score would stand at 506 (or 507 if they made one overtrick.) A successful effort by his (N/S) Team would yield a score of 502 — and that was not enough. Now the goal was to set the opponents — which was a very daunting prospect! What followed was one of the most intricate finessing combinations yours truly has ever seen.

South opened with the heart seven, drawing the three, Ace, and two. The King immediately followed. (Everyone threw low cards.) The ten of Hearts was then trotted out, as West hoped for a lucky ruff by his partner. Instead, East covered North's Jack with his Queen, and South trumped with the three. The first crossroad had been reached, and South realized that if either opponent held a minor suit Ace, the "jig" was up! accordingly, the King of diamonds was played, and it drew three small cards. Next came the club King, with identical results. Realizing that his partner held these Aces, South further analyzed the position. East's one bid was probably based on a natural trump trick. With a holding of Jack fifth (Jxxxx), East's opening bid called for "two"; thus the conclusion was made that he held Jack fourth. A natural trump trick (J 10 9 8) not possible (the eight was in South's hand); therefore, the only chance was to maneuver a repeated finesse.

Eschewing the trump suit for the moment, South led the diamond two, and North was in with the Ace. Now it was his turn to analyze the situation. Why did his partner lead the minor suit Kings so early in the hand? Why did his partner delay the lead of trump? Perhaps, South wanted a trump lead for a finesse. Thus, he opted for the lead of his lowest spade, and East played the Jack, which was taken by the Ace. (West's hand, at this point, was immaterial — but his diamond discard verified South's suspicions.). The trump position was now clear, and a low club was led to North — who won his Ace. A second spade drew the ten, as South won the King. Hoping for a miracle, South played his last club, and his prayer was answered when North produced the Queen, and led his last trump. East was thoroughly skewered, as he held the nine-seven in front of the Queen-eight. In desperation, he tried the seven — but South was in full control, and the eight was finessed. The balance of the hand was claimed, as the Queen extracted East's beleaguered nine.

Thus, the E/W contract was scuttled, and N/S won the game! An observer asked South — "what if East had played the SEVEN of spades on the first round of trump?" South replied, "I would have played the EIGHT of spades, for a "deep" finesse, and then cashed the top three spades — dropping the J-10-9!"

Do you believe South? Would you buy a used car from him? I guess we will never know, as East chose to cover with his higher Spades at every opportunity. It was still a most interesting hand. . . .

ILLUSTRATIVE HAND #24 — "WATCH THOSE SPOTS"

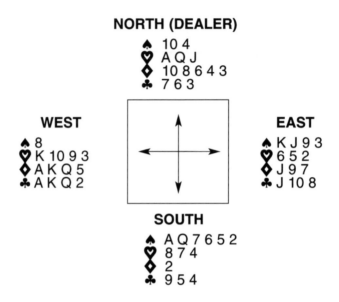

NORTH (DEALER)
♠ 10 4
♥ A Q J
♦ 10 8 6 4 3
♣ 7 6 3

WEST
♠ 8
♥ K 10 9 3
♦ A K Q 5
♣ A K Q 2

EAST
♠ K J 9 3
♥ 6 5 2
♦ J 9 7
♣ J 10 8

SOUTH
♠ A Q 7 6 5 2
♥ 8 7 4
♦ 2
♣ 9 5 4

BIDDING (SCORE: N/S 442 – E/W 446)

EAST	SOUTH	WEST	NORTH
2	4	4	2

Whoever said little cards were useless? The management of the "spot" cards in the trump suit by the North/South Team is a joy to behold! These plays are the signature of great partnerships. Once again, it was another tight battle, as both sides were within range of victory. East opened with a two bid, and his spades certainly justified it. South, with a long and somewhat decent trump suit, inserted a bid of four. West had a pretty darn nice hand himself, and bid a four of his own — with the threat of a possible win. Now North had to decide to go for the set of stretch a bid of three from his heart values. After all, if the finesse was on side, the suit could cash for three tricks. He opted to bid a safe two, and leave the option for the set. If his side made THEIR contract of six and defeated the opponents, they would win the game! It was an ambitious but reasonable plan.

East led his club eight, South played low, and West won the Queen. Everyone followed low, and two more high clubs were cashed. Pleased with his first three tricks, West correctly eschewed leading the thirteenth club (it would not have helped, as South had the last play). Instead the diamond King was led, as low spots were played by all, and the suit was continued with the Ace. It was trumped with the deuce, as West sighed disappointment. Still, his side had four tricks in the bank, and his partner had bid two. . . .

South, now on lead, pondered the possibilities. More information was needed, and the heart suit remained unexplored; thus the heart four was played. West hesitated momentarily, and followed with the ten. North now took stock of the situation. Surely his partner's bid was based on a long trump suit. If said spade suit was solid, then he certainly would have bid five or six. What justified East's two bid? It was not the minor suits, as West had already showed great strength in clubs and diamonds. West had "hitched" on the heart lead, most likely showing the King. (East would not have counted an unprotected King of Hearts as part of his bid, anyway.). Therefore East had some spade length and probably a few trump honor cards as well. Therefore, a trump lead would prove very helpful to partner. The immediate decision was the heart finesse, and the Jack was inserted — holding the trick, as expected. Now the spade ten came from North's hand — a very critical card indeed! East quickly covered with the Jack. South played the Queen, and noted the fall of the eight from the West hand. The seemingly small detail decided the outcome of the hand.

The heart seven now landed on the table, and West played low, as North repeated the finesse — winning the Queen. The lowly spade four was played, and East brilliantly, without the slightest pause, dropped the three! South countered magnificently with the seven — a wonderful read of the spots — based on the previous fall of the eight. If West had scored this trick with the nine (assuming he held this card), that would leave the King singleton, and a very easy drop under the Ace when South regained the lead. In the game of Bridge, this is referred to as a "safety play". It was rather obvious to East/West that their opponents were very seasoned.

Now the trump Ace was cashed — felling the nine, as West and North discarded their lowest diamonds. South then exited with a small heart, and North grabbed his well-preserved Ace. Another diamond was led. East would eventually take his Master Trump, but North and South were certain of making their bid. Best of all, East/West were held to five tricks. A truly wonderful hand — and first rate play on both sides!

ILLUSTRATIVE HAND #25 — "CRACKING UNDER THE PRESSURE"

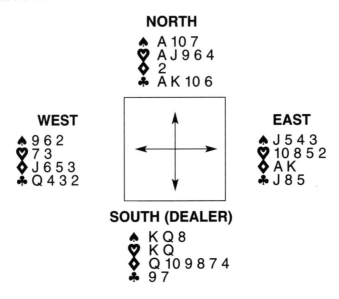

NORTH
♠ A 10 7
♥ A J 9 6 4
♦ 2
♣ A K 10 6

WEST
♠ 9 6 2
♥ 7 3
♦ J 6 5 3
♣ Q 4 3 2

EAST
♠ J 5 4 3
♥ 10 8 5 2
♦ A K
♣ J 8 5

SOUTH (DEALER)
♠ K Q 8
♥ K Q
♦ Q 10 9 8 7 4
♣ 9 7

BIDDING (SCORE: N/S 394 – E/W 373)

WEST	NORTH	EAST	SOUTH
NIL	5	3	3

This most extraordinary hand was observed during the Playoff Rounds in the Zone for the Las Vegas Grand Prix Qualifier (February 1999). West opened with a Nil bid, which had a very high percentage probability. The only risk was the spade nine; however, the low spots offered excellent discarding opportunities. North came in with a very sound bid of five (especially after the Nil call). East decided to go for the win with a three bid, as he calculated that 130 points would be sufficient. South took the safety of a three bid of his own. (Bidding any higher than four would have been inane!) It was quite obvious that a set of the Nil was in order, as the East bid appeared to be a sure thing. It came down to a very tense ending, and East, with victory in his grasp fumbled the ball at the goal line!

West led the diamond six to East's King and South's seven. The diamond Ace now appeared, and it was followed by the nine, Jack and the spade seven (ruff) by North. The Ace of hearts was cashed, as East played the deuce, and South dropped the King. West's heart suit was safe, and he happily threw the seven. The four of hearts fetched South's Queen, as East and West pitched low spot cards. Now South dropped the nine of clubs on the table, as West followed with the four, while North played the King, and East deposited the five. The Ace of clubs drew the eight, the seven (completing the "high-low" signal), and the Queen from a very happy West.

The club ten was covered by the Jack, as South ruffed with the spade King — a very farsighted play. The diamond Queen was a logical choice, as West had to play low, and North trumped rather extravagantly with the Ace of spades. (East discarded a low heart). The six of clubs drew another heart discard from East, as South ruffed with the trump Queen and West tossed his last club. The ten of diamonds extracted West's last spot card, and North trumped with his spade ten, which forced an underruff by East. (The spade Jack had to be saved for possible protection for his partner.) This fascinating position had been reached:

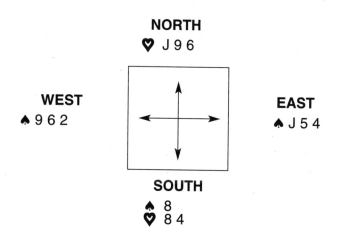

NORTH
♥ J 9 6

WEST
♠ 9 6 2

EAST
♠ J 5 4

SOUTH
♠ 8
♥ 8 4

The innocent-looking layout has a devilish trap. Do you see the danger after North leads any heart? In any case here is what happened:

The heart Jack was correctly trumped with the spade four. Had East ruffed high, South would have ditched his eight of trump, transposing to the actual outcome. Now South properly released the diamond eight, as West was forced to play the trump two. East found himself at the crossroads and decided that the natural play of spade Jack was quite irresistible. After all, who could have argued with logic? He later said that he was afraid that the lead of the five might have pinned a trick on his partner — but he did not analyze the actual possibilities. Had West held the NINE and EIGHT of trump, the hand was lost anyway; If South actually held the NINE and EIGHT of trump, then it did not matter which card he (East) led. Therefore, the scenario of these two specific trump DIVIDED between the West and South hands had to be considered. Since it was obvious that West would not have bid Nil with a suspect spade suit, he had to hold reasonably safe trump and the SIX was probably in his hand as well. Thus the Jack would allow South to unload his high spade!

It is truly amazing how much analysis can be wrung out of this seemingly basic position!

Therefore, the unusual lead of the spade five was clearly indicated. (Then the Jack picks up the nine at the end.) The five forces the eight from South, and allows West to unblock his six. Reverse the nine and eight, and if South holds the nine, this permits West to discard his eightspot.

The premature lead of the Jack is the"kiss of death" to West, as it smothers both the nine and eight and promotes the lowly six to a winner!

Poor East! He worked so hard — only to become an unexpected ally to North and South — and helped to break his partner's Nil! Did he "crack" under the pressure? Perhaps his impulse to make the "text" play can be forgiven. After all, would you have led the FIVE in the critical position?

I hope that you have enjoyed this book, and improved your game. I want to thank the many contributors of ideas, suggestions, and material for the Revised Edition. If you have any comments or want to inquire about the Tournaments and the National Card Players' Organization, please contact me at this e-mail address: heartsmoon@aol.com. Good luck at your next on-line or live Tournament!

— Joe ("Bartbear") Andrews